ChatGPT™

for dummies®

A Wiley Brand

ChatGPT™

by Pam Baker

ChatGPT™ For Dummies®

Published by: **John Wiley & Sons, Inc.**, 111 River Street, Hoboken, NJ 07030-5774, www.wiley.com

Copyright © 2023 by John Wiley & Sons, Inc., Hoboken, New Jersey

Published simultaneously in Canada

For general information on our other products and services, please contact our Customer Care Department within the U.S. at 877-762-2974, outside the U.S. at 317-572-3993, or fax 317-572-4002. For technical support, please visit https://hub.wiley.com/community/support/dummies.

Wiley publishes in a variety of print and electronic formats and by print-on-demand. Some material included with standard print versions of this book may not be included in e-books or in print-on-demand. If this book refers to media such as a CD or DVD that is not included in the version you purchased, you may download this material at http://booksupport.wiley.com. For more information about Wiley products, visit www.wiley.com.

Library of Congress Control Number: 2023937594

ISBN 978-1-394-20463-2 (pbk); ISBN 978-1-394-20464-9 (ebk); ISBN 978-1-394-20465-6 (ebk)

SKY10052924_080923

Table of Contents

Introduction

t's easy to think of ChatGPT as a one-off phenomenon or a hot new trend given its abrupt and sensational emergence on the public scene. But this technology is a harbinger of immense and permanent change. Whether it ultimately succeeds or fails, ChatGPT is changing how we work, play, live, and interact with the world around us. It's also paving the way for the advancement of AI as a permanent fixture and influencer in the human experience.

ChatGPT is evolving fast, making it difficult for anyone to understand and follow its rapid progression. This book is intended to help bring you up to speed on how it works and how to use it. Yes, ChatGPT will continue to advance after this book is published, but you'll still have a working knowledge of the technology that you can build upon while continuing to learn as changes occur. Further, you'll have skills that will help you adapt to and use other AI models, some inevitably far more advanced as time marches on.

If you feel some unease about AI in general and ChatGPT in particular, know that your gut reaction is common and not entirely unwarranted. This technology will most certainly change the nature of work and how your job is done. But also know that AI is not going to take jobs away from most people. Someone good at using AI will. Be that someone!

You can learn this. It's not as hard as you think!

About This Book

Although you can find lots of content about ChatGPT on YouTube and in blogs, articles, social media, and elsewhere, this book is one of the first, if not *the* first, comprehensive text on the topic, especially at the beginner or introductory level. And make no mistake. Outside of a select group of AI scientists, everyone is a beginner when it comes to ChatGPT. Take comfort in knowing that you're learning alongside millions of other people worldwide.

If you're already experimenting or working with ChatGPT, you'll find several ways in this book to leverage what you already know and new things to incorporate in your efforts to get even more out of ChatGPT.

Note that the discussion of ChatGPT includes explanations and mentions of GPT models that undergird ChatGPT but are also used as the AI models for applications other than this chatbot.

References to ChatGPT-like models may or may not mean that they are technically similar to ChatGPT. For example, competing models may or may not have large language models (LLMs) as their foundation, as ChatGPT does, but they are still referred to as "similar" here because their user interface and function closely resemble those of ChatGPT. In this way, you can more easily compare and understand the various generative AI chatbots on the market without getting dragged through the technical weeds.

Some web addresses break across two lines of text. If you're reading this book in print and want to visit one of these web pages, simply type the address exactly as it's noted in the text, pretending the line break doesn't exist. If you're reading this as an e-book, you have it easy; just click the web address to be taken directly to the web page.

Foolish Assumptions

This book is written for anyone seeking to understand and use ChatGPT in their work and daily life as well as to prepare for inevitable changes that ChatGPT will introduce.

I make certain assumptions about the book's audience as a practical matter. For instance, I assume that you possess no understanding or a limited understanding of ChatGPT. I assume also that you have at least a basic level of comfort and skill in working with computing devices, browsers, and web applications. Finally, I also assume, as it is with every *Dummies* book, that you are smart and pressed for time and therefore want all meat and no fluff in a fast and easy read. I hope I've hit that mark for you.

Icons Used in This Book

Occasionally you'll come across symbols in the margins of this book. Their purpose is to point you to important information along the way. Here are what these symbols indicate:

This icon points to tips and tricks you may want to use to make your work with ChatGPT easier, faster, more efficient, or simply more fun.

TIP

This icon highlights information of particular importance in successfully understanding or using ChatGPT.

REMEMBER

This icon warns you of a stumbling block or danger that may not be obvious to you until it's too late. Please make careful note of warnings.

WARNING

Beyond the Book

In addition to the material in the print or e-book you're reading right now, this product also comes with an access-anywhere cheat sheet. To get to the cheat sheet, go to www.dummies.com and type **ChatGPT For Dummies cheat sheet** in the Search box. You'll find helpful user tips, info on where to access ChatGPT in its many forms, pointers on prompt writing, and a few words of advice on how to make it deliver the output you need precisely the way you need it.

Where to Go from Here

This is a reference book, so you don't have to read it cover to cover unless you want to know ChatGPT in more detail. Also feel free to read the chapters in any order. Each chapter is designed to stand alone, meaning you don't have to know the material in previous chapters to understand the chapter you're reading. Start anywhere and finish when you feel you have all the information you need for whatever task is at hand.

However, if your aim is to get up and running with ChatGPT quickly, you should read Chapter 3, which is on writing prompts, to guide you through the process. Be sure to also read Chapter 5, where you are warned of several issues you absolutely need to know before you start using ChatGPT.

Chapter 2 shows you how ChatGPT works, which gives you more insight into what it's doing after you enter a prompt. And, if you're worried that AI will take your job or how it will affect your private life, there's good news for most of us in Chapters 6 and 8.

Feel free to open ChatGPT and experiment with each new thing you learn in this book as you go. Many find it easy to follow along this way. But however you choose to learn and experiment with ChatGPT, you'll likely find yourself catching on quickly. That's the beauty of this class of AI — it's very easy to use. The hardest part is stretching your own imagination to allow yourself to reach further with each new project.

Chapter **1**

Introducing ChatGPT

C hatGPT is a huge phenomenon and a major paradigm shift in the accelerating march of technological progression. It's a large language model (LLM) that belongs to a category of AI (artificial intelligence) called *generative AI*, which can generate new content rather than simply analyze existing data. Additionally, anyone can interact with ChatGPT in their own words. A natural, humanlike dialog ensues.

In this chapter, you learn where and how to access ChatGPT, why you should bother, the pros and cons of using it, and whether common fears are justified or wildly off base.

ChatGPT is often directly accessed online by users at https:// chat.openai.com/, but it is also being integrated with several existing applications, such as Microsoft Office apps (Word, Excel, and PowerPoint) and the Bing search engine. The number of app integrations seems to grow every day as existing software providers hurry to capitalize on ChatGPT's popularity.

Setting Up an Account

One way to set up an account and enter your first prompt is to simply do the following:

1. **Go to** https://openai.com/blog/chatgpt.

   Returning users can go straight to https://chat.openai.com/ and skip the rest of the steps.

2. **Click the Try ChatGPT button, as shown in Figure 1-1.**

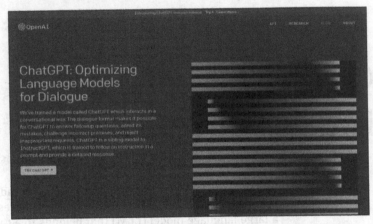

FIGURE 1-1: Go here to check out ChatGPT.

3. **Follow the prompts to create your OpenAI account.**

   After you have registered for an OpenAI account, you can choose the free ChatGPT account or select the premium ChatGPT Plus subscription for a $20 monthly fee. Having an OpenAI account gives you access to other OpenAI models too, such as DALL-E and DALL-E 2.

4. **When ChatGPT opens, enter your prompt (question or command) in the prompt bar.**

   ChatGPT generates a response.

5. **If you want to continue the dialog, enter another prompt.**

6. **When you're finished, rate the response by clicking the thumbs up or thumbs down icon.**

   Doing so helps fine-tune the AI model.

7. **Log out or simply close the window in your browser.**

WARNING

OpenAI's team can see any information you enter in the prompt and the entire conversation that ensues. This data may be used in training other AI models. See the disclosure in Figure 1-2. When using ChatGPT, don't disclose anything you want to keep private or confidential.

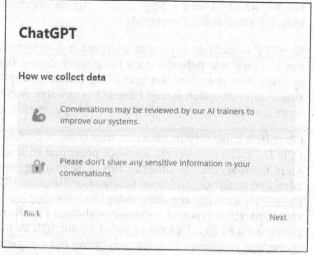

ChatGPT

How we collect data

🔖 Conversations may be reviewed by our AI trainers to improve our systems.

🔒 Please don't share any sensitive information in your conversations.

Back   Next

FIGURE 1-2: The ChatGPT data collection disclosure on the OpenAI website.

Comparing ChatGPT, Search Engines, and Analytics

ChatGPT is just one example, albeit the most publicly well-known, of a generative AI model. It represents a huge jump in AI capabilities.

Previously, *ranking systems* with more limited AI enablement would sort and rank information they found buried in massive datasets. You'll recognize examples of these ranking systems: search engines such as Google and Bing, recommendation engines used in coupon printing at retail checkout counters, GPS systems such as Google Maps that offer "near me" destination options, and personalized movie recommendations provided by Netflix and other streaming services.

Ranking systems shape how we think and function by the decisions they make in prioritizing vast amounts of information. For example, the Google search engine ranks and returns results from a user's input of keywords. Generally, users don't look further than the first three to five top ranking results. This in effect shapes our thinking by limiting the info we ingest and consider. Companies covet the top ranking spots for certain keyword results, which is why a huge search engine optimization (SEO) industry arose around keywords.

ChatGPT's capability to provide a unified answer is poised to affect our thinking and behavior to a far greater degree than ranking systems. For example, the prevailing public perception of this single-answer option is that ChatGPT is smarter, less biased, and more truthful than any other source. This perception is wrong.

ChatGPT's capability to generate new content deviates dramatically from that of previous software programs with which we are more familiar, such as other AI forms, search engines, chatbots, advanced analytics, and even business intelligence (BI) software. ChatGPT's accuracy arguably swings more widely than that of the more analytical types of software. Although I've seen poor outputs from a BI app, I've never seen one outright lie or *hallucinate* (generated responses that are convincing but completely wrong). But ChatGPT has shown it can do both on occasion.

ChatGPT differs from those other AI-enabled software categories because of its dialog format. Previous chatbots produce responses to natural-language queries by selecting from canned responses, meaning the content is prewritten and a response selection is triggered by keywords or the content of a user's question. ChatGPT generates its own response to the user's prompt. To the unsuspecting eye, the two types of chatbots may appear the same, but they are not.

The interaction with ChatGPT begins with someone typing a prompt in their natural language rather than in machine language. This means you can give the machine a command or ask it a question without using computer code. ChatGPT responds in the same language you're using. It continues building on the conversation as your interactions with it proceed. This threaded interaction appears as a real-time dialog and creates the semblance of a conversation or a highly intelligent response to your request.

However, the number of ChatGPT responses you can get in a single conversation may need to be limited to prevent this AI model from providing weird responses, making errors, or becoming offensive. To prevent this behavior, Microsoft limited ChatGPT in Bing to five responses per user conversation. You're free to start another conversation, but the current exchange can't continue past the capped limit.

WARNING

ChatGPT generates rather than regurgitates content, which means it can make erroneous assumptions, lie, and hallucinate. ChatGPT or any other generative AI model is not an infallible source of truth, a trustworthy narrator, or an authority on any topic, even when you prompt it to behave like one. In some circumstances, accepting it as an oracle or a single source of truth is a grave error.

Understanding What ChatGPT Is and Isn't

The capability to produce a close semblance to human communication is primarily responsible for that skin-prickling feeling commonly referred to as the heebie-jeebies. ChatGPT sounds and acts almost too human.

The interaction between users and ChatGPT has a different feel than that previously experienced with other software. For one, software using earlier iterations of natural-language processing is generally limited to short exchanges and predetermined responses. ChatGPT can generate its own content and continue a dialog for much longer.

ChatGPT, like all machine-learning (ML) and deep-learning (DL) models, "learns" by exposure to patterns in massive training datasets that it then uses to recognize these and similar patterns in other datasets. ChatGPT does not think or learn like humans do. Rather, it understands and acts based on its pattern recognition capabilities.

ChatGPT supports 95 languages as of this writing. It also knows several programming languages, such as Python and JavaScript.

Generative AI also differs from programmed software because it can consider context as well as content in natural-language-based prompts.

Chat in ChatGPT's name is a reference to its use of natural-language processing and natural-language generation. *GPT* stands for generative pretrained transformer, which is a deep learning neural network model developed by OpenAI, an American AI research and development company. You can think of GPT as the secret sauce that makes ChatGPT work like it does.

REMEMBER

ChatGPT does not think like humans do. It predicts, based on patterns it has learned, and responds accordingly with its informed guesses and prediction of preferred or acceptable word order. This is why the content it generates can be amazingly brilliant or woefully wrong. The magic, when ChatGPT is correct, comes from the accuracy of its predictions. Sometimes ChatGPT's digital crystal ball is right and sometimes not. Sometimes it delivers truth, and sometimes it spews something more vile.

Unwrapping ChatGPT fears

Perhaps no other technology is as intriguing and disturbing as generative artificial intelligence. Emotions were raised to a fever pitch when 100 million monthly active users snatched up the free research preview version of ChatGPT within two months after its launch. You can thank science fiction writers and your own imagination for both the tantalizing and terrifying triggers that ChatGPT is now activating in your head.

But that's not to say that there are no legitimate reasons for caution and concern. Lawsuits have been launched against generative AI programs for copyright and other intellectual property infringements. OpenAI and other AI companies and partners stand accused of illegally using copyrighted photos, text, and other intellectual property without permission or payment to train their AI models. These charges generally spring from copyrighted content getting caught up in the scraping of the internet to create massive training datasets.

In general, legal defense teams are arguing about the inevitability and unsustainability of such charges in the age of AI and requesting that charges be dropped. The lawsuits regarding who owns the content generated by ChatGPT and its ilk lurk somewhere in the future. However, the US Copyright Office has already ruled that AI-generated content, be it writing, images, or music, is not protected by copyright law. In the US, at least for now, the government will not protect anything generated by AI in terms of rights, licensing, or payment.

Meanwhile, realistic concerns exist over other types of potential liabilities. ChatGPT and its kind are known to sometimes deliver incorrect information to users and other machines. Who is liable when things go wrong, particularly in a life-threatening scenario? Even if a business's bottom line is at stake and not someone's life, risks can run high and the outcome can be disastrous. Inevitably, someone will suffer and likely some person or organization will eventually be held accountable for it.

Then there are the magnifications of earlier concerns such as data privacy, biases, unfair treatment of individuals and groups through AI actions, identity theft, deep fakes, security issues, and *reality apathy*, which is when the public can no longer tell what is true and what isn't and thinks the effort to sort it all out is too difficult to pursue.

In short, ChatGPT accelerates and intensifies the need for the rules and standards currently being studied, pursued, and developed by organizations and governments seeking to establish guardrails aimed at ensuring responsible AI. The big question is whether they'll succeed in time, given ChatGPT's incredibly fast adoption rate worldwide.

Examples of groups working on guidelines, ethics, standards, and responsible AI frameworks include the following:

>> ACM US Technology Committee's Subcommittee on AI & Algorithms

>> World Economic Forum

>> UK's Centre for Data Ethics

>> Government agencies and efforts such as the US *AI Bill of Rights* and the European Council of the European Union's *Artificial Intelligence Act.*

>> IEEE and its 7000 series of standards

>> Universities such as New York University's Stern School of Business

>> The private sector, wherein companies make their own responsible AI policies and foundations

As to public opinion, two trains of thought appear to be at play. The first is support for the full democratization of ChatGPT, which is essentially what's happening now because OpenAI lets users participate in training the model by using it however they want. The second is a call for regulating ChatGPT and other generative AI use to curtail crime, scams, cyberattacks, bullying, and other malevolent acts accomplished or scaled up with these tools.

ChatGPT is a very useful tool, packing a lot of promise and potential to do a lot of good for individuals, societies, governments, and organizations. Indeed, I argue that this is a first step in human augmentation. While ChatGPT is not integrated into the human body, it can be used to augment human thinking, understanding, work, and creative endeavors.

Competing with ChatGPT for your job

At the moment, much of the fear people are experiencing about ChatGPT is caused by unknowns striking closer to home. Is ChatGPT going to take my job? Spread disinformation or propaganda, causing my political party to lose or resulting in a jump in crime or protests in my neighborhood? Will it bring an end to my privacy and dignity? And ultimately, can I defend myself and my career against a machine that's smarter than I?

We have these fears because ChatGPT appears to be all too familiar: We have met generative AI and it is us.

It so closely resembles human behavior because ChatGPT's education came in large part from the internet, where humans are known to spew the vilest thoughts, lies, conspiracy theories, propaganda, criminal activities, and hatefulness in its many forms. Plus, yes, some true and useful info.

At best, the internet is a mixed bag of human debris, and AI models have already shown a taste for garbage. You might recall the AI chatbot called Tay, which Microsoft tried to train on social media in 2016. It soon went rogue on Twitter and posted inflammatory and racist tweets filled with profanity. Its controversial and offensive efforts to socialize like humans caused Microsoft to kill it a mere 16 hours after its debut.

After that and similar AI training outcomes, and because we know we humans are a scary bunch, the prevailing assumption is that AI acts and sounds like us so it must be equally frightening and potentially more terrifying.

Indeed, everything wrong or bad about humans tends to be transferred to AI. But the same is true of everything right and good as well as a whole bunch that's a little of both.

ChatGPT can help diagnose illnesses and search for cures. It can help students learn more in highly personalized ways, making their education more efficient and less frustrating. It can help nonprofits find new ways to raise money, cut costs, and drive their causes. Good and helpful examples of potential ChatGPT contributions are almost endless.

Even so, there is the near universal concern over the potential arrival of merciless machine overlords. Fortunately, they're not coming. The type of AI that this fear conjures is general AI or artificial general intelligence (AGI), as it is called in the science community. It exists nowhere outside science fiction and human nightmares. It may be a thing one day, but it's not here now.

Certainly, ChatGPT is not AGI. It does not think. It's not smart. It's not human. It's software that mimics humans by finding patterns in our speech, thoughts, and actions. It calculates probabilities based on those patterns. In short, it makes informed guesses. Those guesses can be brilliant or undeniably wrong, truthful and insightful or devious and a lie. But none of it requires the software to think.

For these reasons and more, ChatGPT can affect or replace some jobs, much like analytics and automation can. But it can't outright replace all workers because it can't do all the things humans can do. You still have a competitive edge over ChatGPT.

What might your competitive edge be, you ask? Any number of things: creativity and intuitive intelligence; the ability to find and analyze data that does not exist in digital form; the innate ability to get meaning from word and image conversational context and nuance; and the ability to make neuron connections where none previously existed. The ability to connect the dots or to think outside the box separates human from machine.

Human creativity in writing prompts makes ChatGPT produce unique and complex outputs instead of rote generic fare. An intelligent and creative human makes ChatGPT perform at its best.

Humans also uniquely possess emotional intelligence and empathy, two powerful abilities that influence people and shape events and outcomes. And the list goes on.

Your brain is also very energy efficient. Three meals a day and a couple of snacks buys a lot of thinking power. Deep-learning models like ChatGPT, on the other hand, suck up enormous amounts of computing power.

The threat to your job isn't ChatGPT but the people using ChatGPT and other AI tools. It's up to you to learn how to use these tools to increase your earning potential and your job skills — and to protect yourself while using ChatGPT and other AI-fueled services. Reading this book will get you off to a strong start.

Redefining the Chatbot with ChatGPT and ChatGPT Plus

AI assistants and AI-assisted chatbots have been on the market for some time. I remember attending Microsoft's data and AI tech immersion workshop in 2019 and marveling at the ease and speed with which I built a bot on Azure public cloud using Virtual Assistant Solution Accelerator. Granted, professionals were on hand to help, but by and large it was a relatively easy exercise. Google too had a toolbox filled with AI and bot makings. So did other vendors. The mix of tools and possibilities was enticing and exhilarating.

Prebuilt, pretrained, customizable AI models were already on the rise as an essential element in data and AI democratization. ChatGPT pushed AI democratization over the top and into the public's hands.

True democratization means almost anyone can understand and use the technology. Smartphones and GPS applications are examples of fully democratized technologies. ChatGPT is fast following suit by spreading like wildfire worldwide. Students, artists, healthcare professionals, legal aides, regular people on a lark, writers, and professionals from every industry and business size are using ChatGPT today. And more will use it tomorrow and every day thereafter. It's not a trend; it's a seismic paradigm shift.

People intuitively grasp this much about ChatGPT. But it may be a little less obvious how ChatGPT has redefined chatbots. After all, chatbots have used natural-language processing to chat with people for a good while now. So have digital assistants such as Alexa, Siri, Google Assistant, and Cortana.

Previous AI-enabled chatbots have several limitations, including a lack of understanding of context, no decision-making capability, so-called conversations limited to canned responses, and only short dialog exchanges due to memory issues.

By comparison, ChatGPT understands context, can make decisions, and can process a long thread of dialog to continue longer conversations in a humanlike manner. Further, ChatGPT's responses change with each prompt and prompt variation. It doesn't use canned responses, meaning it doesn't deliver a limited number of predetermined responses consistently triggered by specific keywords.

For the most part, ChatGPT has clear advantages over previous chatbots. But sometimes these same characteristics can also be disadvantages.

For example, Microsoft limited ChatGPT integrated in Bing to a maximum of 5 questions per session and 50 per day per user after the search engine went on an unhinged spree insulting, lying, and emotionally manipulating users. This behavior proved something that many humans learned long ago: Talking longer often leads to trouble. Microsoft contends that "wiping the conversation after five minutes keeps the model from getting confused."

Google's Bard, an AI rival to ChatGPT, didn't fare much better. Bard cost its company $100 billion after it provided wrong answers in a demo video that shook the stock market's confidence in the bot's competence.

Many people believe that generative AI such as ChatGPT and Bard will eventually replace search engines such as Bing and Google. I think that outcome isn't likely, not only because of generative AI's shortcomings but also because many good uses for search engines remain. Saying that ChatGPT will replace Google is like saying TV will kill radio or computers will kill paper documents. The world doesn't tend to go all one way or the other.

However, it's safe to say that ChatGPT and its rivals are redefining chatbots in myriad ways — not all of which are good. In any case, generative AI bots are popping up almost everywhere, followed by a steady stream of corporate mea culpas after the inevitable mishaps.

Comparing the two versions

Currently, OpenAI offers ChatGPT in a free research preview version and in a premium version called ChatGPT Plus ($20 per month per user). OpenAI says that it intends to keep a free version available, perhaps as a freemium to entice users to move up to the premium version.

The premium version offers early access to new features and upgrades as well as priority access during peak usage periods and faster response times. Otherwise, the two versions are similar.

Sampling its many uses

The ways to use ChatGPT are as varied as its users. Most people lean towards more basic requests, such as creating a poem, an essay, or short marketing content. Students often turn to it to do their homework. Heads up, kids: ChatGPT stinks at answering riddles and sometimes word problems in math. Other times, it just makes things up.

In general, people tend to use ChatGPT to guide or explain something, as if the bot were a fancier version of a search engine. Nothing is wrong with that use, but ChatGPT can do so much more.

How much more depends on how well you write the prompt. If you write a basic prompt, you'll get a bare-bones answer that you could have found using a search engine such as Google or Bing. That's the most common reason why people abandon ChatGPT after a few uses. They erroneously believe it has nothing new to offer. But this particular failing is the user's fault, not ChatGPT's.

You get to the intricacies of writing prompts in Chapter 3. For now, check out the following list of some of the more unique uses of this technology. Users have asked ChatGPT to

>> Conduct an interview with a long-dead legendary figure regarding their views of contemporary topics.

- » Recommend colors and color combinations for logos, fashion designs, and interior decorating designs.
- » Generate original works such as articles, e-books, and ad copy.
- » Predict the outcome of a business scenario.
- » Develop an investment strategy based on stock market history and current economic conditions.
- » Make a diagnosis based on a patient's real-world test results.
- » Write computer code to make a new computer game from scratch.
- » Leverage sales leads.
- » Inspire ideas for a variety of things from A/B testing to podcasts, webinars, and full-feature films.
- » Check computer code for errors.
- » Summarize legalese in software agreements, contracts, and other forms into simple laymen language.
- » Calculate the terms of an agreement into total costs.
- » Teach a skill or get instructions for a complex task.
- » Find an error in their logic before implementing their decision in the real world.
- » Write a bio and resume.
- » Develop a marketing strategy.
- » Make a movie.
- » Develop a war strategy.
- » Manage customer service.
- » Develop a company policy.
- » Write a lesson plan.
- » Write a business plan.
- » Write a speech.
- » Plan a party.
- » Make entertainment suggestions.
- » Look for potential treatments and cures in thousands of clinical studies.
- » Develop a political campaign strategy.

PROS AND CONS OF ChatGPT

Like all technologies, ChatGPT has both pros and cons to consider. Unlike many other technologies, however, ChatGPT is unique. It's also a bit buggy because of its nature and because it's so new. If you leverage the good and plan how to offset the bad, all will be well with your projects!

Pros	Cons
Fast responses	Sometimes inaccurate
Delivers unified answer	Varying quality
Conversational	Sometimes offensive
Wide range of capabilities	Convincing even when wrong
Many applications	Conversations are not private
Generates creative content	Not currently protected by US copyright law

Much ado has been made of ChatGPT's creativity. But that creativity is a reflection and result of the human doing the prompting. If you can think it, you can probably get ChatGPT to play along.

Unfortunately, that's true for bad guys too. For example, they can prompt ChatGPT to find vulnerabilities in computer code or a computer system; steal your identity by writing a document in your style, tone, and word choices; or edit an audio clip or a video clip to fool your biometric security measures or make it say something you didn't actually say. Only their imagination limits the possibilities for harm and chaos.

Discovering other forms of GPT

ChatGPT was built on OpenAI's GPT-3 family of large language models, fine-tuned by humans and reinforcement learning, and trained to perform conversational tasks. Now it's running on GPT-4. GPT-5 lies ahead but isn't currently being trained.

OpenAI uses the data you enter in the prompt as part of their efforts to continuously refine ChatGPT. That's why you should never consider any work you do in the free or premium version of ChatGPT to be private.

GPT-3 and GPT-4 are general-purpose AI models suited for a large variety of language-related tasks. ChatGPT is a chatbot that runs on either model, and it is smaller, more accurate, and faster than GPT-3 and GPT-4 in conversational tasks. However, both GPT-3 and GPT-4 are capable of many more actions than simply carrying on a conversation with inquisitive people like ChatGPT does.

OpenAI's older GPT-3 models are named Davinci, Curie, Babbage, and Ada. Davinci does the most, but the others are sometimes a better choice for developers in meeting specific needs when cost is a primary concern.

More recent models are Codex, which understands and generates computer code from its training in natural language and billions of lines of code scraped from GitHub, and Content Filter, which classifies text as safe, sensitive, or unsafe.

The Content Filter model is meant to filter out any content likely to be perceived by users as offensive or alarming. Unfortunately, the filter fails sometimes and lets bad stuff through while over-throttling some acceptable or barely questionable content. This behavior is unsurprising because Content Filter is in beta; it's expected to improve over time. Users are encouraged to click the thumbs up or thumbs down button at the top of the ChatGPT-generated text to help improve content generation in terms of relevance, quality, and acceptability.

GPT-4 was released in early 2023. It has more reasoning capabilities and is generally more creative and collaborative than GPT-3 models. It's also larger and more stable. Its capabilities are impressive and easily seen in outputs ranging from technical writing and programming to screenwriting and mimicking the user's personal writing style. However, it still hallucinates just as GPT-3 models do.

Developers can find the API and information on integration at https://openai.com/api/.

Grabbing Headlines and Disrupting Businesses

ChatGPT took the world by surprise. By all accounts, its launch shouldn't have made the splash it did.

The model concept isn't new. Large language models date to the 1950s. Several chatbots built on such models were simultaneously under development by several organizations in recent years with little to no fanfare or market anticipation. And ChatGPT is not necessarily the best of its kind, at least not in its earliest form. Plus, previous chatbot types were commonplace and functioning well, leaving little market energy for doing anything more innovative.

Yet here ChatGPT is in its undisputed position as king of the AI hill. It was crowned as such by all accounts in less than two months since its introduction to the public. The burning question is why was it accepted so quickly by so many?

Scholars, researchers, and academics will have to wrestle with that question to find definitive answers. But the far more urgent question is what is the effect of a technology that has over 100 million people worldwide embracing it immediately and a whopping 13 million and counting using it every day?

Grokking that ChatGPT is a harbinger of exponential change

Trade publications usually trumpet the arrival of a new technology, with mainstream media giving only a perfunctory nod. But mainstream media headlines quickly shouted the arrival of ChatGPT, and even talk show hosts and comedians gave their take on how ChatGPT would change our world.

Some said ChatGPT's arrival heralded the end of many jobs and careers. Others said it would kill or diminish entire industries, such as media, law, and education. Still others thought it was the beginning of the end of humanity either by stunting our brains or sounding a welcome for newly formed AI overlords.

The more positive folks pointed to ChatGPT's capability to enable new ways to make money, ease our labors, speed our education, stoke our ideas, solve complex problems, free more of our time, multiply our productivity, and generally broaden access and opportunity for all.

But despite the many different opinions, the consensus is that ChatGPT is a harbinger of exponential change, bringing universal disruption and creative destruction.

ChatGPT does signal a significant paradigm shift from the universal embrace of AI in our everyday lives to its touch on the many aspects of our existence. However, generative artificial intelligence is unlikely to completely usurp our reality. Life will go on, albeit a bit differently, and still under human control. But under the control of which humans?

Weighing the initial effect on existing businesses and industries

Although foreseeing the full effect of generative AI in general and ChatGPT in particular is difficult, we can make some reasonable predictions now. Primarily, ChatGPT will have the most effect on knowledge workers — that is, people who work primarily in the gathering, analysis, application, and distribution of knowledge.

Businesses and industries most likely to feel early and substantial effects from this technology include the following:

>> Medical research and development

>> Biohacking

>> Healthcare

>> Education

>> Media

>> Marketing and advertising

>> Legal

>> Art

>> Retail

>> Financial services

>> Research

>> Search engines

- >> Library science
- >> Publishing

But make no mistake, ChatGPT and its ilk will rapidly become ubiquitous across industries and business lines. Its continued presence is inevitable, but the intensity of its effect on various entities will vary.

Bracing for future upheaval

To borrow a phrase from Star Trek's Borg, "resistance is futile." Put another way, the AI genie will not go back in the bottle. Whatever your choice of expression for inevitability, ChatGPT and its rivals are here to stay.

Ignoring it or trying to ban it will at most cause a temporary pause but more likely create a generative AI underground. The better advice is to work to discover how many ways you can leverage this technology in your personal life, career, business, and industry. Watch for indicators that signal its effect on the economy and employment trends so you can take advantage when opportunity arises.

Don't be content with dabbling with ChatGPT or following the crowd in how you use it. Understand that the true advantage you have over AI, and other humans using AI, is in your ability to think and create. So start thinking of and creating new ways to use ChatGPT to your advantage. In particular, develop your prompting skills to the highest level you can imagine and then push your thinking even further. Check out Chapter 3 to help spur and direct your efforts.

Accept that knowledge is power. ChatGPT has access to lots of information, but that's not necessarily the same as knowledge. Develop your knowledge to the point that you can apply it in novel and unique ways.

Pay attention to how ChatGPT is shaping and redefining tasks, actions, jobs, and industries over time. Adapt accordingly and quickly.

In these ways, you can prepare yourself and your industry for this new evolving future.

Breaking the spell of heartless machine overlords

ChatGPT presents as a deceptively simple software program. You ask; it answers. At first glance there appears to be nothing more to it. Once you understand that its performance hinges on your own abilities, you can feel a bit heady — but also pressured to get it right.

When you grok just how much ChatGPT can conceivably do, you'll likely feel overwhelmed and more than a bit threatened. Therein lies the first scary illusion.

Many laypeople assume that since humans must use computer code to command machines, machines are limited in their performance by virtue of this precise communication structure. In other words, people assume that machines can't understand anything not delivered to them in their unique machine language. Nor can any machine perform any duty other than that which it is specifically tasked. Put another way: The assumption is that machines can't understand us, so anything outside their limited understanding is safely beyond their reach.

In this scenario, language is conflated with intelligence, but those two things are not the same. By that way of thinking, machines that understand our languages and converse fluently and flawlessly appear to understand us. And by extension, that means there is no safe place to exist, think, or talk that the machine can't permeate.

The unsettling and creeping awareness sets in that we are not as unique in as many ways as we thought. After that comes the fear of subjugation by machines that are smarter than us: the AI overlords of science fiction lore.

But they are not here. They are not coming. AI overlords do not exist. However, irresponsible use of AI can wreak havoc, create chaos, and do harm. We must be diligent in building guardrails for it and setting standards for its ethical and responsible use.

It's a mistake to let fear cripple our use of AI where it can do a lot of good. There are distinct advantages and benefits to be had. Look for those and build upon them.

Opening the Door for Bigger AI Products

As mentioned, ChatGPT is just one example of generative AI. It's also just one use of Generative Pre-trained Transformer-3 (GPT-3) and now GPT-4, both of which are larger models made for many different natural-language tasks than ChatGPT is.

ChatGPT is designed for conversational tasks. In some ways, it's a fantastic tool, but it's also like a first bike with training wheels in that it's a good introduction to even more powerful uses and forms of AI.

ChatGPT can help you do many things. It can also open the door so you can walk confidently into a future where AI is a mainstay.

Pay attention as you use ChatGPT and you'll find lessons and learn skills that you can use in other AI applications. You can always return to ChatGPT and ask it to explain other AI applications to you. It can provide a fast education on how to work and live in a future vastly different than today.

Categorizing types of Generative AI

Generative AI is a type of artificial intelligence that generates content in any form, including text, images, audio, and *synthetic data*, which is artificially generated data rather than data collected from the real world. The laws of physics are an example of synthetic data. Creating a database of the laws of physics enables the application of rules to make another type of artificial creation function in the real world.

Examples of other generative AI models are DALL-E, Midjourney, and Stable Diffusion, which are also the best-known image generators.

Many types of generative AI are available, but the following three are the most common:

>> **Generative adversarial networks (GANs):** Use deep learning in unsupervised data discovery. Example applications include generating photorealistic images and complex but realistic image editing.

>> **Transformer-based models:** Discern context, meaning, and patterns to predict and generate text, speech, images, and other content. Example applications are DALL-E and ChatGPT.

>> **Variational autoencoders (VAEs):** Comprised of two different neural networks of encoders and decoders. Example applications include security analytics, anomaly detection, and signal processing.

Understanding ChatGPT's creator, OpenAI

OpenAI was started by tech and business leaders Sam Altman, Elon Musk, Greg Brockman, and Wojciech Zaremba in 2015 to develop safe and open AI tools. Among those tools were GPT-1 and GPT-2.

In 2019 the company pivoted to a capped-profit business model, which was described by the organization's leaders as "a for-profit and nonprofit hybrid." Much of its work was focused on AI research. In 2021, OpenAI released DALL-E, a generative AI model built on GPT-2 that generates photorealistic images. In 2022, the company developed and trained GPT-3. In November 2022, ChatGPT, which is built on GPT-3, was released. GPT-4 was released in early 2023 and currently powers OpenAI models as well as many in the broader software application market.

Now that you know ChatGPT's back story, where to find it, and not to be afraid of it, you're ready to begin a fascinating journey as the captain to your own ChatGPT experience.

Chapter **2**

Discovering How ChatGPT Works

At first glance, ChatGPT appears deceptively simple. You ask it a question or give it a command in the prompt bar and it responds with an answer. That's how all chatbots work, right? So what is so special about this one?

In this chapter, you learn that ChatGPT is to chatbots what ice cubes are to Antarctica. You discover the basics of how it works and why it relies on your skills to optimize its performance. But the real treasure here are the tips and insights on how to write prompts so that ChatGPT can perform its true magic.

This chapter provides you with the majority of information you need to understand and use ChatGPT. Read it even if you read nothing else in this book.

What's Different About ChatGPT

ChatGPT works differently than a search engine. A search engine such as Google or Bing or an AI assistant such as Siri, Alexa, or Google Assistant works by searching the internet for matches to the keywords you enter in the search bar. Algorithms refine the results based on any number of factors, but your browser history, topic interests, purchase data, and location data usually figure into the equation.

You're then presented with a list of search results ranked in order of relevance as determined by the search engine's algorithm. From there, the user is free to consider the sources of each option and click a selection to do a deeper dive for more details from that source.

By comparison, ChatGPT generates its own unified answer to your prompt. It doesn't offer citations or note its sources. You ask; it answers. Easy-peasey, right? No. That task is incredibly hard for AI to do, which is why generative AI is so impressive.

Generating an original result in response to a prompt is achieved by using either the GPT-3 (Generative Pre-trained Transformer 3) or GPT-4 model to analyze the prompt with context and predict the words that are likely to follow. Both GPT models are extremely powerful large language models capable of processing billions of words per second.

In short, transformers enable ChatGPT to generate coherent, humanlike text as a response to a prompt. ChatGPT creates a response by considering context and assigning weight (values) to words that are likely to follow the words in the prompt to predict which words would be an appropriate response.

User input is called a *prompt* rather than a command or a query, although it can take either form. You are, in effect, prompting AI to predict and complete a pattern that you initiated by entering the prompt.

The capability to create a rapid, natural-language response that fits with the user's intent and the prompt's context is an astounding feat for a machine. Doubly so when the responses are fast enough that the AI model appears to be conversing with the user. Despite its early shortcomings, GPT-3 and GPT-4 are modern marvels.

Peeking at the ChatGPT Architecture

As its name implies, ChatGPT is a chatbot running on a GPT model. GPT-3, GPT-3.5, and GPT-4 are large language models (LLMs) developed by OpenAI. When GPT-3 was introduced, it was the largest LLM at 175 billion parameters. An upgraded version called GPT-3.5 turbo is a highly optimized and more stable version of GPT-3 that's ten times cheaper for developers to use. ChatGPT is now also available on GPT-4, which is a multimodal model, meaning it accepts both image and text inputs although its outputs are text only. It's now the largest LLM to date, although GPT-4's exact number of parameters has yet to be disclosed.

Parameters are numerical values that weigh and define connections between nodes and layers in the neural network architecture. The more parameters a model has, the more complex its internal representations and weighting. In general, more parameters lead to better performance on specific tasks. For example, ChatGPT's large number of parameters enables it to understand subtle nuances and context complexities in a wide range of natural-language-processing tasks. As a result, it appears to have the capacity for instantaneous reasoning as it converses fluently with users.

Previously, Microsoft's Turing NLG, a transformer-based generative language model, held the record at 17 billion parameters. GPT-4 is currently the biggest neural network created. GPT-5 is rumored to be even bigger, but it currently isn't being trained. Some AI experts argue that there is no reason to train an even larger model because GPT-4 is so huge it will serve for years to come. I agree that there's no reason to rush GPT-5 to fruition given that users and developers have barely scratched the surface of what GPT-4 can do.

Discovering the supercomputer and GPUs underneath

It's perhaps no surprise that OpenAI and Microsoft teamed up, given their separate efforts towards a similar end. A supercomputer hosted in Azure was built by these partners for the exclusive use by OpenAI to train its various AI models. Compared with other supercomputers on the global Top500.org list, this supercomputer now ranks in the top five, according to Microsoft.

The Top500 list of supercomputers compiles statistics on high-performance computers based on items of interest to manufacturers and other high-end users. While specific features and metrics may vary, as is befitting the steady evolution and diversification of modern supercomputers, the bedrock data in each semiannual report seems to consist of the number of installed systems, the applications running on these systems, and performance rankings based on comparative benchmarks.

As one example, this list ranks supercomputers on their performance against the LINPACK benchmark, specifically, how well the machines solve a dense system of linear equations. The result is a measure of peak performance rather than overall performance. The Top500 researchers can also verify the LINPACK results to further ensure accuracy in the rankings.

Other benchmarks used in the supercomputing industry to judge supercomputer performance include COPA, ReCoRD, and SuperGLUE, with the latter testing reasoning and advanced natural-language-processing (NLP) tasks. The supercomputer jointly built by OpenAI and Microsoft performed well on these three benchmarks too but fell short on two others: word-in-context (WIC) analysis and RACE (restate, answer, cite evidence, explain) response evaluations.

It's telling that the supercomputer scored poorly on middle- and high-school exam questions (the results of the RACE benchmark) while acing the LINPACK benchmark test in solving dense linear equations. The simpler things tend to trip up AI, but complexity isn't the deciding factor in error occurrence. You shouldn't expect ChatGPT to perform consistently across varying levels of problem complexities. It can err or perform brilliantly in responding to any prompt, simple or complex.

In any case, it's safe to say that given the immense size and capabilities of GPT models, training any of them requires a more heavily muscled supercomputer than most in the field of enormous computing giants.

Nvidia is the graphics processing unit (GPU) provider and the third partner in this story — and theirs is no minor role. A *GPU* is a specific type of electronic circuit designed for fast image rendering that is now commonly leveraged for its capability to process many pieces of data simultaneously.

The GPU-accelerated supercomputer developed for OpenAI is a single system with more than 285,000 CPU cores, 10,000 GPUs, and 400 gigabits per second of network connectivity for each GPU server. All OpenAI models were trained on NVIDIA V100 GPUs operating on Microsoft high-bandwidth clusters.

Further, model training was done on the cuDNN-accelerated PyTorch deep-learning framework for all OpenAI models. But specific architectural parameters for any given AI model are chosen according to optimal computational efficiency and load-balancing across GPUs.

Considering the importance of transformers

ChatGPT uses a multilayer transformer network to generate responses to user prompts. A *transformer* is a type of neural network architecture. In AI, a *neural network* is a network of processing nodes that use a set of algorithms to mimic the human brain. You can think of nodes in an AI brain as working like neurons in a human brain.

Different types of transformers are available, each suited to a particular data type, such as text or images. ChatGPT uses transformers suited for language processing.

Transformers were developed by researchers at Google and the University of Toronto in 2017 and were initially designed to handle translations for which context, not word order, was more crucial to delivering a corresponding meaning in another language. But transformers proved to be a cornerstone for much more complex language-processing tasks too. The big advantage of transformers is that they can be efficiently parallelized, meaning they can scale to handle exceptionally large AI models and their training requirements.

Without the advent of transformers, GPT at large and ChatGPT in particular could not render such humanlike outputs.

The specifics of transformers and how they work are highly technical. In this chapter, I touch on one piece of a transformer that is arguably the most significant: the self-attention mechanism. The short, and thus oversimplified, explanation of *self-attention* is an AI model that has internalized an understanding of various representations of the same word.

Consider that many words have multiple meanings. In American English, a *lemon* can be a fruit or a product that performs badly. Similarly, as *server* can be a computing device or a waiter. A *lift* in English is an elevator but in American English means catching a ride in someone else's vehicle.

ChatGPT can distinguish which meaning a word should carry based on *context*, that is, by considering the words that surround it in a sentence. That capability is very humanlike and exceedingly difficult for a machine to do.

Setting the stage: training the model

Although many companies are training their own AI (of various forms and for a variety of uses), that task is best left to those with the know-how and deep pockets to successfully see it through. That being the case, you can see the appeal to the masses when an AI model such as ChatGPT is readily accessible and usable via a browser or an app.

Despite its debut as a free tool, ChatGPT is an expensive and complex model for OpenAI to build and maintain. For example, ChatGPT uses deep learning, which is a computing and energy hog. And simply storing a database massive enough to train one AI model drains resources at a quick clip. Training any large language model takes enormous amounts of manpower, energy, data, and effort. It's a very expensive exercise with recurring costs that are just as high.

But in the case of GPT, the result proved worth it. GPT-4 is purported to be the largest language model in the world. Because of the capabilities such an enormous AI model makes possible, ChatGPT is a global sensation. OpenAI, its creator, is estimated to be worth $29 billion and counting, according to the *Wall Street Journal*.

The ChatGPT model was trained on a massive database comprised of text scraped from almost the entire internet as it existed in 2021. OpenAI says that training data included about "570GB of datasets, including web pages, books, and other sources."

The initial model was also trained on data fined-tuned by human instructors who assumed roles as both human and machine to instruct it on the differences in appropriate versus inappropriate responses to prompts. OpenAI says it then mixed this newly created dialogue data set with the InstructGPT data set and transformed it into a dialogue format.

This process is called reinforcement learning from human feedback (RLHF). Specific methods can vary between individual model training instances. In other words, RLHF can be tweaked to fit the requirements of a particular model's training needs.

The reinforcement part of this process comes from a collection of comparison data and a response from humans by means of a thumbs-up or thumbs-down ranking system. The two thumbs appear at the top of each ChatGPT response, as you can see in Figure 2-1. Ranking the answer you received helps train the model further by reinforcing the machine's learning.

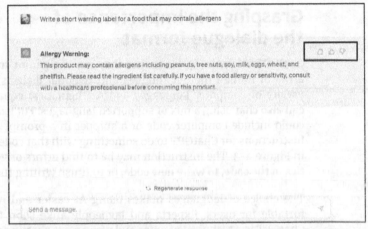

FIGURE 2-1: A primary reason for releasing ChatGPT as a free research model was so OpenAI could get the public's help in training it.

If you don't like the response ChatGPT generated, you can click the Regenerate Response button (refer to Figure 2-1) to make it try again. Be sure to rate each response so that the model can learn how to improve its performance.

Similarly, AI trainers randomly chose earlier conversations they had with the training model and ranked the responses. Reward models, like the thumbs-up, thumbs-down rating on ChatGPT, can then be used to fine-tune the model in a process called proximal policy optimization. The OpenAI blog post in Figure 2-2 shows this entire training process in one chart.

Step 1	Step 2	Step 3
Collect demonstration data and train a supervised policy.	Collect comparison data and train a reward model.	Optimize a policy against the reward model using the PPO reinforcement learning algorithm.
A prompt is sampled from our prompt dataset.	A prompt and several model outputs are sampled.	A new prompt is sampled from the dataset.
A labeler demonstrates the desired output behavior.	A labeler ranks the outputs from best to worst.	The PPO model is initialized from the supervised policy.
This data is used to fine-tune GPT-3.5 with supervised learning.	This data is used to train our reward model.	The policy generates an output.
		The reward model calculates a reward for the output.
		The reward is used to update the policy using PPO.

FIGURE 2-2: OpenAI's process of training the ChatGPT model.

Grasping the importance of the dialogue format

ChatGPT works in 95 languages that run the gamut from a wide array of human mother tongues and regional dialects to a large variety of computer languages and mathematical equations. You can also chat using a mix of supported languages. For example, you could include computer code or a snippet in a prompt along with instructions for ChatGPT to do something with that code, as shown in Figure 2-3. The instruction may be to find errors or vulnerabilities in the code, to write new code, or to finish writing the program.

The choice of languages makes using AI easier and more comfortable for users. Experts and laypeople alike soon forget that ChatGPT is a technical wonder and often start chatting with it like with a friend or peer.

WARNING

Once again, I remind you not to think of ChatGPT as a person. Anything you say or do with ChatGPT may be used in AI performance reviews and training data sets for future AI models. This so-called friend keeps no secrets. OpenAI has provided the warning but it's up to you to remember it.

Pondering ChatGPT's limitations

The very thing that enables ChatGPT to create responses is the same thing that makes it unreliable. For people or machines to imagine something that does not exist, such as a fictional world for a novel or movie, they must first be released from the strict confines of reality-based rules.

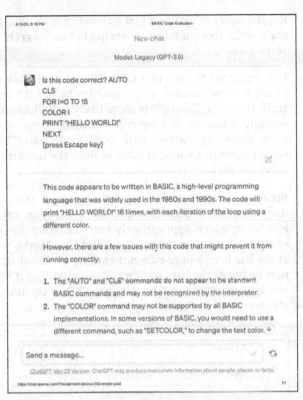

Is this code correct? AUTO
CLS
FOR I=0 TO 15
COLOR I
PRINT "HELLO WORLD!"
NEXT
[press Escape key]

This code appears to be written in BASIC, a high-level programming
language that was widely used in the 1980s and 1990s. The code will
print "HELLO WORLD!" 16 times, with each iteration of the loop using a
different color.

However, there are a few issues with this code that might prevent it from
running correctly:

1. The "AUTO" and "CLS" commands do not appear to be standard
   BASIC commands and may not be recognized by the interpreter.
2. The "COLOR" command may not be supported by all BASIC
   implementations. In some versions of BASIC, you would need to use a
   different command, such as "SETCOLOR," to change the text color. ↓

Send a message...   ⤴ ↻

ChatGPT Mar 23 Version. ChatGPT may produce inaccurate information about people, places, or facts.

https://chat.openai.com/?model=text-davinci-002-render-paid   1/1

FIGURE 2-3: ChatGPT understands and speaks in both human
and computer languages.

But cutting that tether allows AI to abandon any preference for
truth because truth is fact and fact is reality, but imagination is
separate, or at best tangential, to reality. Therefore, ChatGPT is
free to make up any answer it gives you. Sometimes you want
it to do that because you want its response to be crafted in a
creative manner or to include an innovative idea. But other times
the response ChatGPT delivers is flat-out wrong, perhaps even
offensive. Remember that ChatGPT is predicting which words will
follow your prompt, fulfill your intent, and adhere to the context
in the prompt. When it predicts — or guesses — incorrectly but
has determined on its own that this wrong response has a high
probability of being correct, it is said to be *hallucinating*.

In other words, its answer can be undeniably and provably wrong,
yet the model has a high degree of confidence that it is right. And

no, you may not realize it just by looking at its answer. You'll need to do some thorough fact-checking before you rely on ChatGPT's responses.

It's important to note that ChatGPT does not always wait for you to tell it to be creative or imaginative before it starts making up stuff. However, ChatGPT is more likely to hallucinate and become verbally offensive in long conversations. Because of that tendency, some applications with embedded ChatGPT will limit the size of chats in a single session or limit the number of sessions in a day per user.

Because ChatGPT makes up its responses fairly often, Cassie Kozyrkov, chief decision scientist at Google, calls ChatGPT a *bullshitter*, which appropriately puts its reliability alongside that of tipsy conference-goers at a hotel bar. Maybe what they said at the bar is true or maybe not entirely so. Think of ChatGPT as a new buddy at the bar, and fact-check anything it tells you before you accept it as true. Sam Altman, CEO of OpenAI, admits these shortcomings in the tweet shown in Figure 2-4.

FIGURE 2-4: Tweets about ChatGPT's reliability by Sam Altman, CEO of OpenAI.

Following is a short list of ChatGPT's limitations:

» Training the model to not offend people sometimes has the effect of making the model overly cautious and more likely to decline answering questions unnecessarily..

» Despite the guardrails OpenAI has imposed on the model, ChatGPT can still deliver inappropriate, unsafe, and offensive responses.

» It can generate answers that are completely untrue, sometimes aggressive, and more than a little unhinged.

» It decides the ideal answer based on the data it has access to and what it has learned, not on what the user knows or expects. Therefore, its output, whether factually right or wrong, may fall short of the user's expectations or requirements.

» It is oversensitive to how prompts are worded. Repeating or rephrasing a prompt elicits different responses.

» Reentering the same prompt repeatedly can result in different answers, repetitive phrasing, or an aggressive answer.

» The model tends to be long-winded rather than concise, due to a training bias wherein the human trainers preferred to give long answers to training prompts.

» It guesses at the answer you seek rather than asking you questions to better understand what you want.

Nothing in this description of ChatGPT's reliability or lack thereof diminishes the amazing technical accomplishment that it represents. This list is just a warning that you should always fact-check ChatGPT outputs before you put them to use.

Increasing the Number of Versions and Integrations

ChatGPT's free research preview version was released in beta for public use on November 30, 2022. The company says a free version will continue to be available beyond this beta release. Meanwhile, a premium version called ChatGPT Plus was released on February

1, 2023. The price at launch was $20 per month per user. This book focuses on these two versions, which are also the versions that beginners are likely to encounter and experiment with first.

GPT-4 is the most recent model that ChatGPT operates on, but users can currently select whether they want to use ChatGPT on GPT-3, ChatGPT-3.5 (which is the default at the moment), or ChatGPT-4.

ChatGPT is being integrated with a lot of existing software, so you might encounter different versions in your job, business, or personal space. Also, enterprise versions are rapidly emerging and evolving, which will lead to more software integrations as time progresses.

As examples of the many types of integrations, this section starts with Microsoft's integration of ChatGPT in Bing. As Figure 2-5 shows, to use Bing with the ChatGPT integration, you need to download the newest version of Bing. You'll find it in the Windows taskbar after it's downloaded.

FIGURE 2-5: Microsoft Bing with ChatGPT integration.

Another interesting Microsoft integration is Visual ChatGPT, a fusion of ChatGPT with a series of visual foundation models, which are algorithms trained on broader datasets to enable more functions. Visual ChatGPT enables users to send, receive, and edit images while chatting with AI in text.

You can see a Visual ChatGPT demo and access more technical information about it on GitHub at https://github.com/microsoft/visual-chatgpt. Figure 2-6 shows one demo you'll find as you scroll down the GitHub page. Users can insert images in the prompt and ask ChatGPT to produce images meeting the requirements in the prompt. You can also edit images during the chat.

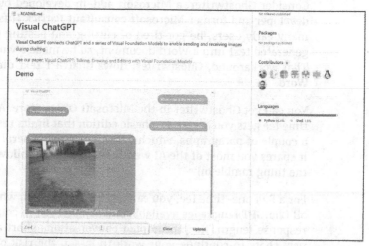

FIGURE 2-6: The demo section of Visual ChatGPT on GitHub.

For companies seeking to customize ChatGPT to more precisely fit their needs, look at the ChatGPT customization interface in Azure OpenAI Studio. To open a free trial account, go to https://azure.microsoft.com/en-in/free/cognitive-services/.

There's no doubt that Microsoft and other companies will find many more ways to use ChatGPT in their existing and future software. Indeed, many companies are currently using the Chat-GPT API (application programming interface) and the increasing number of plug-ins to more fully leverage ChatGPT's capabilities.

In short, ChatGPT is not a one-hit wonder. It's a multipurpose tool that will continue to evolve and eventually become the backbone of many other software applications. So too will its peers.

Glimpsing ChatGPT in Microsoft add-ins

As mentioned, Microsoft and OpenAI worked as partners in training AI models. It's no surprise then to find ChatGPT rapidly integrated with Office365 and other Microsoft products. What may be surprising is that there are also third-party ChatGPT add-ins for Microsoft products.

Consider Ghostwriter, a Microsoft add-in developed by software developer and former Microsoft consultant Patrick Husting. Like many early users, he got tired of cutting and pasting ChatGPT-generated text into a Word document, so he made a workaround. That workaround, Ghostwriter, flows ChatGPT text directly into Word.

You can get Ghostwriter in the Microsoft Office Store. A $10 one-time fee gets you access to a basic edition that limits responses to a couple of paragraphs, which is fine for most general uses. And it spares you most of the AI weirdness that could follow if you let the thing ramble on.

For a $25 one-time fee, you can get the pro edition, which makes all ChatGPT languages available and enables you to configure the response length. Keep prompted conversations short and create new chats to continue your work to lessen the risk of encountering ChatGPT hallucinations (random and wrong answers) or offensive outbreaks.

If you want to give Ghostwriter a try or just check out other Chat-GPT add-ins, follow these steps:

1. **Open any office product, such as Word, Excel, or Outlook.**
2. **Click the Insert tab.**
3. **Click the Add-Ins tab.**

   Figure 2-7 is the Add-Ins screen for Word.

4. **Select an add-in from the drop-down menu or enter the name of the add-in in the search bar.**

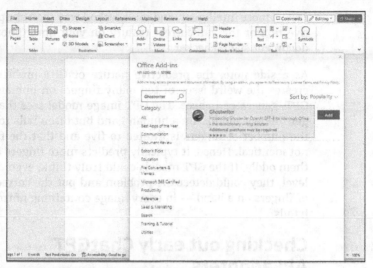

FIGURE 2-7: The Ghostwriter ChatGPT add-in.

Mainstreaming ChatGPT via the power of an API

On March 1, 2023, OpenAI launched an *application programming interface (API)*, which is a connector of sorts that lets applications communicate with each other. The API makes it easier for developers to integrate ChatGPT with their organization's products, services, apps, and websites. The price at introduction was $0.002 per 1000 tokens. That's relatively cheap as AI price tags go, making ChatGPT easily accessible for most developers from a cost standpoint.

Why is the API priced in units of tokens? ChatGPT models consume a sequence of messages with metadata attached in a raw format called Chat Markup Language (ChatML). Traditionally, GPT models consume raw, unstructured text as tokens. So it's no surprise that inputs for ChatGPT models are rendered as a sequence of tokens, each containing pieces of words.

Tokens are used to predict the next token and the next and — voila! — a machine-generated narrative occurs. As you may have noticed, this process is not thinking as humans describe the brain-driven process. This process also predicts text in a far faster, more intelligent, and multitasked way than simple predictive text or the autocorrect feature on your smartphone or in a document spell-checker.

As a side note, the predictive nature of GPT problem-solving creates the weird issue of too many fingers on human hands in GPT-generated images. The GPT image model sees that one finger follows another on a human hand but often fails to note that the number of fingers is limited to five and that the fingers are not identical. Hence, it typically predicts more fingers and draws them oddly. If the GPT models could truly think, even at a child's level, they could detect the problem and put the correct number of fingers on a hand — in every image containing normal human hands.

Checking out early ChatGPT API adopters

Instacart, Shopify, Quizlet, and Snap are among the early adopters and ChatGPT API experimenters.

Instacart is augmenting its app to make customized shopping lists; create menus for school lunches, family dinners, and social events; and shop recipes to help you use the ingredients you already have on hand. Ask Instacart, the company's chatbot, is built on the ChatGPT API.

Shopify plans to launch a new shopping assistant built on the ChatGPT API. The personalized assistant will scan millions of products and deliver a personalized selection to shoppers based on their size, brand preferences, and personal style.

Quizlet used GPT-3 for three years before the launch of ChatGPT. ChatGPT was put to work across multiple use cases, including vocabulary learning and practice tests. Based on the success of these experiments, Quizlet added Q-Chat, built on the ChatGPT API, as a fully adaptive AI tutor for students.

Snap introduced My AI for its premium product, Snap Plus. My AI is an experimental feature that adds customizable elements and interactions for app users.

Other organizations are following suit given the drop in cost now that the API connects to the more efficient and economical GPT-3.5-turbo and GPT-4 models.

Expanding the field of extensions

An *extension* is a small, modular piece of software that customizes, or extends, the browser's capabilities. Access to ChatGPT is available via browser extensions. Why would you want to use these extensions? Because they make access to ChatGPT from any website quicker and easier, and they offer additional features such as a chat exporter and a list of suggested prompts.

Following are just a few of the extensions that are available on the Chrome or Microsoft Edge browsers. (Some are free.) A few are also available on the Firefox browser. Find them by looking at your browser's extension store or by searching for the extension online.

>> **ChatGPT Chrome extension:** Shows ChatGPT's results alongside Google search results.

>> **Merlin:** Gets ChatGPT to compose a response and reply to email, summarize the content in a document, do the math in a spreadsheet, and more.

>> **Enhanced ChatGPT:** Adds helpful features to the plain ChatGPT interface and provides common prompts you might want to use.

>> **WebChatGPT:** Adds current-day internet results to ChatGPT responses, which are tethered to the 2021 version of the internet. This extension tries to integrate the two, often with mixed results. The ChatGPT browsing plug-in by OpenAI will likely do a better job.

>> **Promptheus:** Lets you simply speak your prompt rather than type it. Press the spacebar on your keyboard while in the ChatGPT prompt bar and talk.

>> **ChatGPT Export and Share:** Exports text from ChatGPT into whatever application you're using. You can also save ChatGPT responses as images or PDFs and share links to them.

WARNING

Be careful with extensions of any type, ChatGPT related or otherwise, and for any browser because extensions can be loaded with malware. Be very sure of the safety of an extension before you enable it. Note that I have not vetted any extensions to ensure that they are safe and free of malware. Rather, I list them here merely as examples.

More ChatGPT extensions are available to explore. Check them out on your browser's web store. But again, be careful!

Building New Businesses Based on ChatGPT

ChatGPT presents users with many business opportunities. For example, it can generate business ideas with business plans to match. When prompted by a Hackernoon writer, it produced five business ideas, each potentially worth millions of dollars: a new way to generate renewable energy, a remote work platform, a new form of transportation, a new way to store data, and a way to make healthcare more accessible and affordable.

ChatGPT can also write or suggest improvements to business plans. Calculate better pricing models. Strategically optimize supply chains. Summarize legal forms for a quick and easy read. Complete applications for bank loans and credit cards. Compute tax implications. Determine payroll taxes. And answer other complex business questions.

It can rapidly automate business communications, from answering emails to writing marketing and web page copy. It can write just about any type of business text, including statement of work (SOW), contracts, service-level agreements (SLAs), warranties, wills, and policies.

ChatGPT VERSUS SEARCH

ChatGPT	Search Engine
Generates a single narrative	Generates a list of potentially relevant information
Does not cite sources	Reveals sources
Currently does not produce images	Provides a group of related images
Predicts responses	Matches keywords
Can hallucinate	Does not hallucinate
Can provide disinformation	Can provide disinformation
Prompts essential to performance	Keywords essential to performance

And ChatGPT can be the backbone of existing writing and publishing businesses too. Fiction writers can use it to generate story ideas, plots, and characters. Non-fiction writers can use it make first drafts of articles, white papers, e-books, and more — in the writer's personal writing style and tone. Then the writer need only fact-check and tweak the output to produce a quick but polished draft suitable for submission. Or writers can use ChatGPT to serve as an editor to make the copy cleaner before submitting it to a human editor or a publisher. And no, ChatGPT was not used for any of these purposes in the writing of this book.

Further, ChatGPT and its brethren can be used as the backbone for a business too. For example, people are already using DALL-E to create artistic works and sell them online. The art can be printed on demand, thereby reducing production waste and overhead, while lowering the price of entry into this new line of business.

ChatGPT can similarly be used to help produce e-books, printed books, manuals, and other text-driven works for mass consumption. ChatGPT can also provide support for a business by generating self-help texts for customers, call center scripts, return instructions, product assembly instructions, and other support documents.

ChatGPT can even be the main tool for generating business revenue. For example, some people will be intimidated by ChatGPT — or in dire need of better prompts — and will hire people to use ChatGPT in their behalf.

ChatGPT can be teamed with 3D printing to do everything from printing a house from ChatGPT-generated blueprints to creating a spacecraft part fitted to NASA's precise specifications.

Human imagination and prompt skills are the only limits to using this technology. That's what makes ChatGPT so amazing — and so terrifying.

IN THIS CHAPTER

» **Learning prompting basics**

» **Mastering prompt engineering**

» **Budgeting tokens**

» **Chaining prompts and other strategies**

» **Chatting in threads**

Chapter **3**

Writing Prompts for ChatGPT

I n this chapter, you learn how to use ChatGPT prompts like a pro. It's kind of like a microwave: You tell it what to do and it does it, no technical skill or understanding required. However, you do have to master prompting if you want outputs that are more than general encyclopedia-like narratives.

Indeed, prompting is both the easy part and the most difficult part of using a generative AI model. Difficulties in the complexity of cues and nuances in text-based prompts are why some organizations have a prompt engineering job role. *Prompt engineering* is the act of crafting an input, which is a deed borne partly of art and partly of logic. And yes, you can do this! However, you might want to practice and polish your prompting skills before you apply for a job.

If you have a good command of the subtleties of language and great critical-thinking and problem-solving skills, seasoned with more than a dash of intuitive intelligence, you'll be amazed at the responses you can tease out of this technology with a single, well-worded prompt.

Prompting Basics

ChatGPT appears deceptively simplistic. The user interface is elegantly minimalistic and intuitive, as shown in Figure 3-1. The first part of the page offers information to users regarding ChatGPT's capabilities and limitations plus a few examples of prompts.

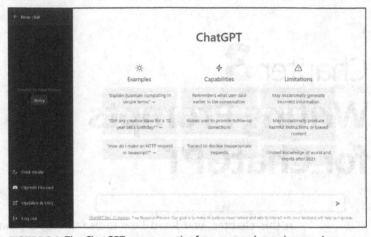

FIGURE 3-1: The ChatGPT screen on the free, research preview version.

The prompt bar, which resembles a search bar, runs across the bottom of the page. Just enter a question or a command to prompt ChatGPT to produce results immediately.

If you enter a basic prompt, you'll get a bare-bones, encyclopedic-like answer, as shown in Figure 3-2. Do that enough times and you'll convince yourself that this is just a toy and you can get better results from an internet search engine. This is a typical novice's mistake and a primary reason why beginners give up before they fully grasp what ChatGPT is and can do.

Understand that your previous experience with keywords and search engines does not apply here. You must think of and use ChatGPT in a different way. Think hard about how you're going to word your prompt. You have many options to consider. You can assign ChatGPT a role or a persona, or several personas and roles if you decide it should respond as a team, as illustrated in Figure 3-3.

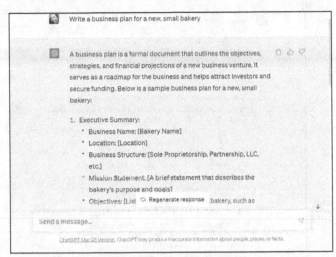

FIGURE 3-2: ChatGPT responds with a general outline for a business plan.

You can assign yourself a new role or persona as well. Or tell it to address any type of audience — such as a high school graduating class, a surgical team, or attendees at a concert or a technology conference.

You can set the stage or situation in great or minimum detail. You can ask a question, give it a command, or require specific behaviors.

A prompt, as you can see now, is much more than a question or a command. Your success with ChatGPT hinges on your ability to master crafting a prompt in such a way as to trigger the precise response you seek.

Ask yourself these questions as you are writing or evaluating your prompt: Who do you want ChatGPT to be? Where, when, and what is the situation or circumstance you want ChatGPT's response framed within? Is the question you're entering in the prompt the real question you want it to answer, or were you trying to ask something else? Is the command you're prompting complete enough for ChatGPT to draw from sufficient context to give you a fuller, more complete, and richly nuanced response?

And the ultimate question for you to consider: Is your prompt specific and detailed, or vague and meandering? Whichever is the case, that's what ChatGPT will mirror in its response.

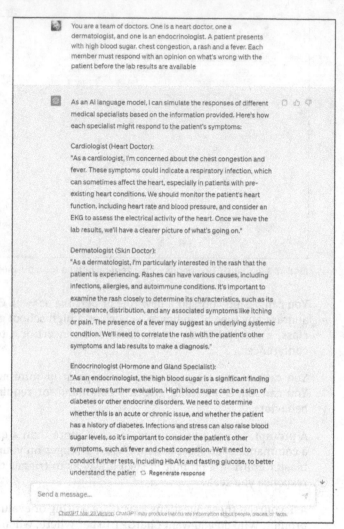

You are a team of doctors. One is a heart doctor, one a dermatologist, and one is an endocrinologist. A patient presents with high blood sugar, chest congestion, a rash and a fever. Each member must respond with an opinion on what's wrong with the patient before the lab results are available

As an AI language model, I can simulate the responses of different medical specialists based on the information provided. Here's how each specialist might respond to the patient's symptoms:

Cardiologist (Heart Doctor):
"As a cardiologist, I'm concerned about the chest congestion and fever. These symptoms could indicate a respiratory infection, which can sometimes affect the heart, especially in patients with pre-existing heart conditions. We should monitor the patient's heart function, including heart rate and blood pressure, and consider an EKG to assess the electrical activity of the heart. Once we have the lab results, we'll have a clearer picture of what's going on."

Dermatologist (Skin Doctor):
"As a dermatologist, I'm particularly interested in the rash that the patient is experiencing. Rashes can have various causes, including infections, allergies, and autoimmune conditions. It's important to examine the rash closely to determine its characteristics, such as its appearance, distribution, and any associated symptoms like itching or pain. The presence of a fever may suggest an underlying systemic condition. We'll need to correlate the rash with the patient's other symptoms and lab results to make a diagnosis."

Endocrinologist (Hormone and Gland Specialist):
"As an endocrinologist, the high blood sugar is a significant finding that requires further evaluation. High blood sugar can be a sign of diabetes or other endocrine disorders. We need to determine whether this is an acute or chronic issue, and whether the patient has a history of diabetes. Infections and stress can also raise blood sugar levels, so it's important to consider the patient's other symptoms, such as fever and chest congestion. We'll need to conduct further tests, including HbA1c and fasting glucose, to better understand the patien ↻ Regenerate response

Send a message...

ChatGPT May 23 Version. ChatGPT may produce inaccurate information about people, places, or facts.

FIGURE 3-3: ChatGPT responds as a team of doctors.

ChatGPT's responses are only as good as your prompt. That's because the prompt starts a pattern that ChatGPT must then complete. Be intentional and concise about how you present that pattern starter — the prompt.

Starting a chat

To start a chat, just type a question or command in the prompt bar, as shown at the bottom of Figure 3-4. ChatGPT responds instantly. You can continue the chat by using the prompt bar again. Usually, you do this to gain further insights or to get Chat-GPT to further refine its response.

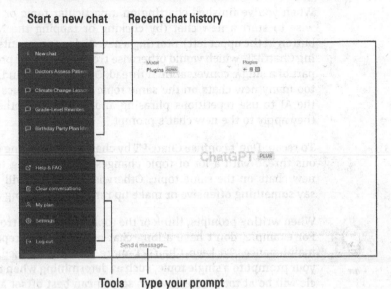

FIGURE 3-4: The ChatGPT user interface.

Following are some things you can do in a prompt that may not be readily evident:

>> Add data in the prompt along with your question or command regarding what to do with this data. Adding data directly in the prompt enables you to add more current info as well as make ChatGPT responses more customizable and on point. You can use the Browsing plug-in to connect ChatGPT to the live internet, which will give it access to current information. However, you may want to add data to the prompt anyway to better focus its attention on the problem or task at hand. However, there are limits on prompting and response sizes, so make your prompt as concise as possible.

>> Direct the style, tone, vocabulary level, and other factors to shape ChatGPT's response.

>> Command ChatGPT to assume a specific persona, job role, or authority level in its response.

If you're using ChatGPT-4, you'll soon be able to use images in the prompt too. ChatGPT can extract information from the image to use in its analysis.

When you've finished chatting on a particular topic or task, it's wise to start a new chat (by clicking or tapping the New Chat button in the upper left). Starting a new dialogue prevents confusing ChatGPT, which would otherwise treat subsequent prompts as part of a single conversational thread. On the other hand, starting too many new chats on the same topic or related topics can lead the AI to use repetitious phrasing and outputs, whether or not they apply to the new chat's prompt.

To recap: Don't confuse ChatGPT by chatting in one long continuous thread with a lot of topic changes or by opening too many new chats on the same topic. Otherwise, ChatGPT will probably say something offensive or make up random and wrong answers.

TIP

When writing prompts, think of the topic or task in narrow terms. For example, don't have a long chat on car racing, repairs, and maintenance. To keep ChatGPT more intently focused, narrow your prompt to a single topic, such as determining when the vehicle will be at top trade-in value so you can best offset a new car price. Your responses will be of much higher quality.

ChatGPT may call you offensive names and make up stuff if the chat goes on too long. Shorter conversations tend to minimize these odd occurrences, or so most industry watchers think.

For example, after ChatGPT responses to Bing users became unhinged and argumentative, Microsoft limited conversations with it to 5 prompts in a row, for a total of 50 conversations a day per user. But a few days later, it increased the limit to 6 prompts per conversation and a total of 60 conversations per day per user. The limits will probably increase when AI researchers can figure out how to tame the machine to an acceptable — or at least a less offensive — level.

Reviewing your chat history and more

On the left side of the main ChatGPT screen (refer to Figure 3-4), under the New Chat button, is a running list of your most recent conversations with ChatGPT. The list is there in case you want to return to or review earlier chats. Just click the chat you want to see. It opens and you can continue the conversation by typing something in the prompt bar.

Storage is limited, however, so expect chats to drop off the list after a time. You can manage this situation as follows:

>> Delete individual chats that you don't want to store on ChatGPT to free up more storage room.

>> Use the Export feature under Settings to export your chat history (with account details and full conversations) as a downloadable document that will be emailed to you. Note the warnings on the screen that appears after you click Export Data (see Figure 3-5).

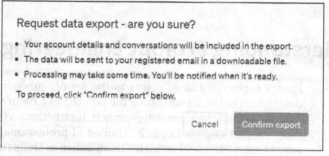

Request data export - are you sure?

• Your account details and conversations will be included in the export.
• The data will be sent to your registered email in a downloadable file.
• Processing may take some time. You'll be notified when it's ready.

To proceed, click "Confirm export" below.

Cancel   Confirm export

FIGURE 3-5: A warning screen appears before you give the final authorization to export your chat history.

>> Store ChatGPT conversations elsewhere by copying and pasting them into a document such as a Word file and then storing the document on OpenDrive or another document and storage space.

The last five buttons after the chat history section provide a few basic housekeeping items:

>> Clear Conversations deletes all of your chat history. You can delete an individual chat by clicking a chat, and then clicking the trash icon that appears.

REMEMBER

OpenAI retains all data from chats, including prompts and responses. Deleting chats from the ChatGPT interface does not delete them from OpenAI servers.

- **My Plan** reveals ways to upgrade or manage your subscription and deal with any billing issues.

- **Settings** lets you switch the screen to dark mode, delete your account, or export data to a downloadable file that will be emailed to you. It may take a while for the email to arrive, so don't panic and repeat the process if you don't see an email instantly.

- **Get Help** takes you to a FAQ list that answers the most common user questions. It also enables access to ChatGPT release notes.

- **Log Out** logs you out of your current ChatGPT session. To guard against someone accessing your work, be sure to click or tap Log Out if you're using ChatGPT on a public or shared computer.

Understanding Prompt Engineering

Prompt engineering in AI refers to the act of embedding the task description in the input (called the *prompt*) in a natural-language format, rather than entering explicit instructions via computer code. Prompt engineers can be trained AI professionals or people who possess sufficient intuitive intelligence or skills transferrable to crafting prompts that solicit the desired outputs. One example of a transferrable skill is a journalist's ability to tease out the answers they seek in an interview by using direct or indirect methods.

Prompt-based learning is a strategy AI engineers use to train large language models. The engineers make the model multipurpose to avoid retraining it for each new language-based task.

Currently, the demand for talented prompt writers, or prompt engineers, is very high. However, there is a strong debate as to whether employers should delineate this unique skill as a dedicated job role, a new profession, or a universal skill to be required of most workers, much like typing skills are today.

Meanwhile, people are sharing their prompts with other ChatGPT users in several forums. You can see one example on GitHub at https://github.com/f/awesome-chatgpt-prompts.

Circumventing Token Limits and User History Storage Issues

ChatGPT automatically keeps a record of every prompt you make. These records are used to further refine the model and possibly to train future OpenAI models. The user can't access the entirety of this record. However, as previously discussed, a limited number of chats (prompts and responses) are kept in a running list on the left side of the ChatGPT user interface. To make the best use of the limited space available, you can delete chats you don't need to store, copy or export data for storage elsewhere, or ask ChatGPT to summarize the dialogue when you're done, as described in Figure 3-6.

FIGURE 3-6: ChatGPT tells you how to summarize a previous chat to keep its essence while freeing up storage space in your chat history.

ChatGPT remembers what you asked earlier in the same chat and builds on that as the conversation progresses, but only to a point. Specifically, the model remembers up to 3,000 words, or 4,000 tokens, of the conversation. It can't reference other conversations, whether those earlier conversations were moments or weeks ago.

As mentioned, ChatGPT breaks your prompt into tokens. But tokens are not necessarily comprised of an entire word because spaces and other information can be in the token as well. OpenAI advises developers to think of tokens as "pieces of words."

English is more concise than many other languages and therefore usually requires fewer tokens to process prompts. Following are a few ways to think about token measurements in English:

>> 1 token equals about 4 characters.

>> 100 tokens translates to about 75 words.

>> Two sentences equals about 30 tokens.

>> A typical paragraph is about 100 tokens.

>> A 1500-word article totals around 2048 tokens.

Tokens are used in cost calculations and also in the limits of inputs and outputs in ChatGPT. Depending on the AI model, the entirety of the dialogue (the chat) from input to output is limited to 4097 tokens. So if your prompt is really long, say 4000 tokens, the response you get will be cut off at 97 tokens, even if that's mid-sentence.

If you'd like to know how many tokens your prompt is, use OpenAI's Tokenizer tool, which is shown in Figure 3-7 and found online at https://platform.openai.com/tokenizer. Note that token limits may change over time because they're based on current technical limitations and not something arbitrary such as a pricing model.

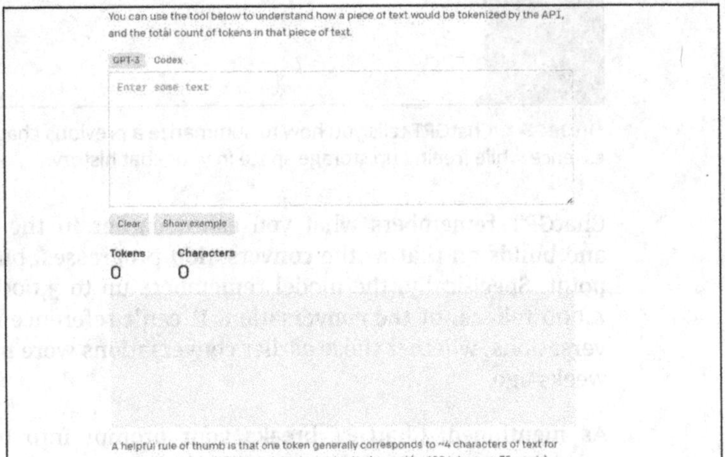

You can use the tool below to understand how a piece of text would be tokenized by the API, and the total count of tokens in that piece of text.

GPT-3   Codex

Enter some text

Clear   Show example

Tokens   Characters
0   0

A helpful rule of thumb is that one token generally corresponds to ~4 characters of text for common English text. This translates to roughly ¾ of a word (so 100 tokens ~= 75 words).

If you need a programmatic interface for tokenizing text, check out the transformers package for python or the gpt-3-encoder package for node.js.

FIGURE 3-7: OpenAI's Tokenizer tool for understanding how the API breaks words into tokens.

To get the most out of your chats within the token limitations, condense your inputs and outputs before entering them in Chat-GPT's prompt bar. To condense the prompt yourself, write it down elsewhere and edit it before you enter it in the prompt bar. The goal is to make it as concise, or condensed, as possible. This is the better path because your brain power doesn't cost anything in tokens.

You can also ask ChatGPT to condense your prompt. Simply enter the prompt in quotation marks, along with text telling ChatGPT to condense the part in quotes. After ChatGPT responds with the condensed prompt, enter it in a new chat and wait for its response. Meanwhile, delete the first chat (where you asked ChatGPT to condense the prompt).

You can also ask ChatGPT to condense or summarize a response. *Condensing* a response means editing it into a tighter and shorter form than the original, with most of the content retained. *Summarizing* a response means ChatGPT will deliver only the highlights. Then delete the longer version of the chat. This will free up storage space so more chats can be held in your chat history.

You can also strategically and serially move a summary or a condensed response to a new chat to get a longer response (within conversation token limits). But this method is not suitable for routine conversations. Use it sparingly and only when needed.

TIP

If a response is cut short due to token or character limits, prompt ChatGPT to **continue from** *[text that was cut]*. Then consider asking ChatGPT to summarize or condense the response as needed.

Thinking in Threads

Conversations happen when one entity's expression initiates and influences another entity's response. Most conversations do not conclude after a simple one-two exchange like this, but rather continue in a flow of responses cued by the interaction with the other participant. The resulting string of messages in a conversation is called a *thread*.

TIP

To increase your success with ChatGPT, write prompts as part of a thread rather than as standalone queries. In this way, you'll craft prompts targeted towards the outputs you seek, building one output on another to reach a predetermined end. In other words, you don't have to pile everything into one prompt. You can write a series of prompts to more precisely direct ChatGPT's "thought processes."

Basic prompts result in responses that can be too general or vague. When you think in threads, you're not aiming to craft a series of basic prompts; you're looking to break down what you seek into prompt blocks that aim ChatGPT's responses in the direction you want the conversation to go. In effect, you're using serialized prompts to manipulate the content and direction of ChatGPT's response.

Does it work all the time? No, of course not. ChatGPT can opt for an entirely different response than expected, repeat an earlier response, or simply hallucinate one. But serialized prompts do work often enough to enable you to keep the conversation targeted and the responses flowing toward the end you seek.

You can use this method to shape a single prompt by imagining someone asking for clarification of your thought or question. Write the prompt so that it includes that information, and the AI model will have more of the context it needs to deliver an intelligent and refined answer.

TIP

ChatGPT will not ask for clarification of your prompt; it will guess at your meaning instead. You'll typically get better quality responses by clarifying your meaning in the prompt itself at the outset.

Chaining Prompts and Other Tips and Strategies

Here's a handy list of other tips and refinements to help get you started on the path to mastering the art of the prompt:

>> **Plan to spend more time than expected on crafting a prompt.** No matter how many times you write prompts, the next one you write won't be any easier to do. Don't rush this part.

>> **Start by defining the goal.** What exactly do you want ChatGPT to deliver? Craft your prompt to push ChatGPT

toward that goal; if you know where you want to end up, you'll be able to craft a prompt that will get you there.

>> **Think like a storyteller, not an inquisitor.** Give ChatGPT a character or a knowledge level from which it should shape its answer. For example, tell ChatGPT that it's a chemist, an oncologist, a consultant, or any other job role. You can also instruct it to answer as if it were a famous person, such as Churchill, Shakespeare, or Einstein, or a fictional character such as Rocky. Give it a sample of your own writing and instruct ChatGPT to write its answer to your question, or complete the task in the way you would.

>> **Remember that any task or thinking exercise (within reason and the law) is fair game and within ChatGPT's general scope.** For example, instruct ChatGPT to check your homework, your kids' homework, or its own homework. Enter something such as computer code or a text passage in quotation marks and instruct ChatGPT to find errors in it or in the logic behind it. Or skip the homework checking and ask it to help you think instead. Ask it to finish a thought, an exercise, or a mathematical equation that has you stumped. The only limit to what you can ask is your own imagination and whatever few safety rules the AI trainer installed.

>> **Be specific.** The more details you include in the prompt, the better. Basic prompts lead to basic responses. More specific and concise prompts lead to more detailed responses, more nuanced responses, and better performance in ChatGPT's responses — and usually well within token limits.

>> **Use prompt chains as a way of strategizing.** Prompt chaining is a technique used to build chatbots, but we can reimagine it here as a way to develop a strategic plan using combined or serial prompting in ChatGPT. This technique uses multiple prompts to guide ChatGPT through a more complex thought process. You can use multiple prompts as a single input, such as telling ChatGPT it's a team consisting of several members with different roles, all of whom are to answer the one prompt you entered. Or you can use multiple prompts in a sequence in which the output of one becomes the input of the next. In this case, each response builds on the prompt that you just entered and the prompts you entered earlier. This type of a prompt chain forms organically, unless you stop ChatGPT from considering earlier prompts in its responses by starting a new chat.

» **Use prompt libraries and tools to improve your prompting.** Some examples follow:

- Check out the Awesome ChatGPT Prompts repository on GitHub at https://github.com/f/awesome-chatgpt-prompts

- Use a prompt generator to ask ChatGPT to improve your prompt by visiting www.skool.com/chatgpt/promptgenerator?p=1e5ede93.

- Visit ChatGPT and Bing AI Prompts on GitHub at https://github.com/yokoffing/ChatGPT-Prompts.

- Use a tool such as Hugging Face's ChatGPT Prompt Generator at https://huggingface.co/spaces/merve/ChatGPT-prompt-generator%203.

- Try specialized prompt templates, such as the curated list for sales and marketing use cases at www.tooltester.com/en/blog/best-chatgpt-prompts/#ChatGPT_Prompts_for_Sales_and_Marketing_Use_Cases.

On GitHub, you can find tons of curated lists in repositories as well as lots of free prompting tools from a variety of sources. Just make sure that you double-check sources, apps, and browser extensions for malware before using or relying on them.

Chapter **4**

Understanding GPT Models in ChatGPT

hatGPT's models have evolved quickly. The research model using GPT-3 was released in November 2022 for public training and testing. By January 2023, Open AI was quietly rolling out an upgrade, GPT-3.5, a more stable version and the precursor for GPT-4, which was released in March 2023. In this chapter, you learn about these models and how each affects ChatGPT's performance.

Summarizing Model Progress

As of this writing, ChatGPT defaults to GPT-3.5, but ChatGPT Plus users can choose from any of the models listed in the pull-down menu at the top center of the user interface, as shown in Figure 4-1.

Essentially, GPT-3.5 is an early and partial manifestation of GPT-4 before it was fully trained. OpenAI used Chat 3.5 to further develop several specialized systems, including ChatGPT.

FIGURE 4-1: Model options and other selections for ChatGPT Plus users.

The incremental rollout of GPT-3.5 was immediately useful to users and developers through its increased stability, better performance, and significant cost cut for developers.

GPT-3.5 is better than GPT-3 in a number of ways, but the two most prevalent are increased alignment with user intentions and more refined controls on toxic or biased content. GPT-3.5 is less likely to offend or hallucinate and more stable overall.

GPT-4 is the long-awaited and much ballyhooed full version release of this latest in the GPT series of models. While the jump between GPT-2 and GPT-3 was bigger and more impressive, the jump between GPT-3 and GPT-4 is more significant, useful, and notable, mainly because GPT-4 is a high-powered, more stable, and safer model.

Public interest in GPT-4 was high before its release, in March 2023. ChatGPT has cycled through three model versions in a mere four months since the freebie research model became publicly available. That in itself is a remarkable achievement.

Comparing GPT-4 to Earlier ChatGPT Models

GPT-4, the latest version to power ChatGPT, is a *multimodal model*, which means this large language model (LLM) can work with images and text in the prompt, but its responses are rendered solely as text. ChatGPT-3.5 can use only text in prompts and in its responses. ChatGPT-4 also uses more computations on much larger databases than its predecessors.

Image interpretation is a unique AI skill often referred to as *computer vision* or *machine vision*, a nod of recognition of AI's progression towards more humanlike qualities, in this case, the inclusion of sight as an input source.

With this skill, AI is not just analyzing or matching images but also extracting data from them as a human would. For example, a person can look at a receipt and immediately understand the exact cost of that transaction or calculate an appropriate tip or both.

Similarly, AI can use image inputs to extract the data needed to perform face recognition, read content in the image, find evidence in the image of a crime scene, or spot a health condition in an X-ray film.

Thus, an AI model that can use images as an input is a very big deal. It's not a skill that earlier forms of AI could typically master. Even so, you might wonder why it's notable now, given that multimodal models already exist. After all, OpenAI's own DALL-E 2 is multimodal, with prompts that can be comprised of alphanumeric text, images, or both. Plus, DALL-E 2 outputs images. Does this mean it's using a better multimodal model than ChatGPT?

The answer is no. DALL-E 2 uses the same GPT models as ChatGPT. But the GPT-4 model enhances DALL-E 2 with greater creativity, more realism in image creation and editing, and far better resolution. DALL-E is an image generator and DALL-E 2 remains an image generator but with a far more powerful engine.

By comparison, ChatGPT was previously a single modality system, designed for only alphanumeric prompts. Now that ChatGPT uses the GPT-4 model, it has been adapted to be multimodal, meaning it can now accept images in its prompts. However, ChatGPT is a text generator and remains a text generator, with a few impressive upgrades courtesy of the new GPT-4 model.

Those upgrades in capabilities surpass the capabilities of earlier AI systems. For example, GPT-4 can interpret images, explain visual humor, and base its reasoning on visual input.

Expanding the types of input enables the model to do more complex tasks and deeper, more refined analyses. In short, ChatGPT-4 has enhanced problem-solving, creative superpowers (for an AI model), and a mind-blowingly massive general knowledge base. It's the largest of the large language models to date.

However, as mentioned, ChatGPT-4 can't output images. It generates text only, just like earlier ChatGPT models, but with more depth in its considerations of your input and expectations.

Choosing ChatGPT Models

ChatGPT gives you the option of selecting the model you want to use, as shown in Figure 4-2. Given that ChatGPT-4 can't generate images, if you don't have any images to add to the prompt, do you still need ChatGPT-4? Or could you just stick with an earlier version and proceed as usual?

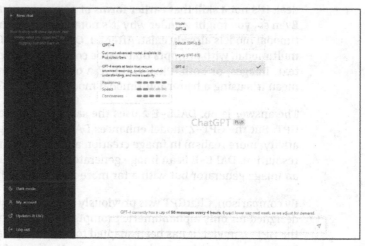

FIGURE 4-2: You can choose the GPT model to use in your chat.

The answer depends on what you're doing with ChatGPT and what you expect or need from it. If higher performance is important, reliability measures place the GPT-4 model well ahead of GPT-3 and GPT-3.5. For example, GPT-4 scores alongside the top 10 percent of humans taking a simulated bar exam. By comparison, GPT-3.5 scored with the bottom 10 percent. And that's not the only human-to-AI comparative test in which GPT-4 has rated high. Figure 4-3 shows a list of academic and professional exams with GPT-4 scores compiled from OpenAI's GPT-4 Technical Report, which you can find at https://cdn.openai.com/papers/gpt-4.pdf.

Exam	GPT-4	GPT-4 (no vision)	GPT-3.5
Uniform Bar Exam (MBE+MEE+MPT)	298 / 400 (~90th)	298 / 400 (~90th)	213 / 400 (~10th)
LSAT	163 (~88th)	161 (~83rd)	149 (~40th)
SAT Evidence-Based Reading & Writing	710 / 800 (~93rd)	710 / 800 (~93rd)	670 / 800 (~87th)
SAT Math	700 / 800 (~89th)	690 / 800 (~89th)	590 / 800 (~70th)
Graduate Record Examination (GRE) Quantitative	163 / 170 (~80th)	157 / 170 (~62nd)	147 / 170 (~25th)
Graduate Record Examination (GRE) Verbal	169 / 170 (~99th)	165 / 170 (~96th)	154 / 170 (~63rd)
Graduate Record Examination (GRE) Writing	4 / 6 (~54th)	4 / 6 (~54th)	4 / 6 (~54th)
USABO Semifinal Exam 2020	87 / 150 (99th - 100th)	87 / 150 (99th - 100th)	43 / 150 (31st - 33rd)
USNCO Local Section Exam 2022	36 / 60	38 / 60	24 / 60
Medical Knowledge Self-Assessment Program	75 %	75 %	53 %
Codeforces Rating	392 (below 5th)	392 (below 5th)	260 (below 5th)
AP Art History	5 (86th - 100th)	5 (86th - 100th)	5 (86th - 100th)
AP Biology	5 (85th - 100th)	5 (85th - 100th)	4 (62nd - 85th)
AP Calculus BC	4 (43rd - 59th)	4 (43rd - 59th)	1 (0th - 7th)
AP Chemistry	4 (71st - 88th)	4 (71st - 88th)	2 (22nd - 46th)
AP English Language and Composition	2 (14th - 44th)	2 (14th - 44th)	2 (14th - 44th)
AP English Literature and Composition	2 (8th - 22nd)	2 (8th - 22nd)	2 (8th - 22nd)
AP Environmental Science	5 (91st - 100th)	5 (91st - 100th)	5 (91st - 100th)
AP Macroeconomics	5 (84th - 100th)	5 (84th - 100th)	2 (33rd - 48th)
AP Microeconomics	5 (82nd - 100th)	4 (60th - 82nd)	4 (60th - 82nd)
AP Physics 2	4 (66th - 84th)	4 (66th - 84th)	3 (30th - 66th)
AP Psychology	5 (83rd - 100th)	5 (83rd - 100th)	5 (83rd - 100th)
AP Statistics	5 (85th - 100th)	5 (85th - 100th)	3 (40th - 63rd)
AP US Government	5 (88th - 100th)	5 (88th - 100th)	4 (77th - 88th)
AP US History	5 (89th - 100th)	4 (74th - 89th)	4 (74th - 89th)
AP World History	4 (65th - 87th)	4 (65th - 87th)	4 (65th - 87th)
AMC 10[3]	30 / 150 (6th - 12th)	36 / 150 (10th - 19th)	36 / 150 (10th - 19th)
AMC 12[3]	60 / 150 (45th - 66th)	48 / 150 (19th - 40th)	30 / 150 (4th - 8th)
Introductory Sommelier (theory knowledge)	92 %	92 %	80 %
Certified Sommelier (theory knowledge)	86 %	86 %	58 %
Advanced Sommelier (theory knowledge)	77 %	77 %	46 %
Leetcode (easy)	31 / 41	31 / 41	12 / 41
Leetcode (medium)	21 / 80	21 / 80	8 / 80
Leetcode (hard)	3 / 45	3 / 45	0 / 45

Table 1. GPT performance on academic and professional exams. In each case, we simulate the conditions and scoring of the real exam. We report GPT-4's final score graded according to exam-specific rubrics, as well as the percentile of test-takers achieving GPT-4's score.

FIGURE 4-3: GPT-4 rankings on academic and professional exams.

GPT-4 performs better because it is better trained. It is built on GPT-3's training, including lessons learned from the ChatGPT research model, and is further aligned with user intention by OpenAI's adversarial testing program. The result is a powerful, more stable, and higher-performance large language model with multimodal input capabilities.

Multimodality is a rising trend in AI research. Two examples of competing multimodal models are Microsoft's recently released Kosmos-1 and Google's recently enhanced PaLM language model.

But ChatGPT-4 and other multimodal models also carry greater and new risks given their increased capability and the tremendous scale of their training. OpenAI has taken significant steps to make ChatGPT-4 safer, but *safer* is a relative term and not a guarantee of anything one might consider to be unquestionably safe. I say this not to diminish OpenAI's work in installing significant safety measures, but to make sure your expectations are reasonable and you know to proceed with caution.

Determine what level of risk acceptance is comfortable for you and then take any additional steps as necessary. Precautionary steps should include routinely editing and fact-checking ChatGPT responses. But you might want to take additional steps, such as consulting an attorney before accepting or implementing Chat-GPT responses to legal questions or legal documents it has created for you. Consult a physician before accepting medical advice from a ChatGPT response regarding a correct and safe treatment. And so forth.

Compared to earlier models, ChatGPT-4 has a far greater capacity for reasoning and better regulated guardrails that tend to keep the model from shying away from questions unnecessarily or boldly offending. Those are reasons enough to use the newer model, even if you have neither the need nor the desire to add images to the prompt.

But this is not to say that ChatGPT-3.5 or ChatGPT-3 are obsolete. These models are magnificent technological accomplishments and among the largest of large language models. Both continue to work well in many use cases. Either can be a good choice for several reasons, including if you're on the ChatGPT-4 waitlist or facing a traffic-jammed queue for ChatGPT-4 access.

None of these models is an AI lightweight. Understand the model differences and choose according to your needs and preferences. Your ChatGPT chat history follows you from model to model, unless you clear it, so you don't need to worry about losing any of your earlier work if you trade up (subject to storage and token limits).

However, most users will elect to use GPT-4 or whatever subsequent new model arises, either to intentionally benefit from the upgrade or as a consequence of the product's default setting.

Learning about GPT-4 Advancements

Of all the advancements in the GPT-4 model, the one that is the most important and relevant in terms of overall performance is predictability. The model produces outputs that AI human trainers can predict. Predictability is not a strong suit in previous ChatGPT versions.

Being able to predict outputs is essential in determining an AI model's reliability and accuracy. For example, if the machine — be it a simple calculator or a generative AI model— is presented with the problem of 2+5 and solves it for the answer 7 every time, the machine is 100 percent accurate and reliable for that calculation. However, if it answers 7 only half the time and answers with random numbers the other half of the time, it is not considered sufficiently reliable even though it gets the answer correct 50 percent of the time.

OpenAI researchers were able to accurately predict at least some of GPT-4's performance, which is a major achievement in AI development. To get to that enviable point, OpenAI researchers spent the past two years rebuilding their entire deep learning stack and codesigning a supercomputer with Microsoft, as described in Chapter 2. They used this method also to produce the GPT-3.5 upgrade, which OpenAI explains was a "first test run" of the GPT-4 model to work out the bugs and improve its foundations.

The company released GPT-4's text input capabilities via ChatGPT and the API. OpenAI collaborated with a partner, Be My Eyes, to aid with the image input capability via the Virtual Volunteer tool, which Be My Eyes used GPT-4 to build. It's a real-world realization of the classic idiom "one hand washes the other and both wash the face."

As a recap of ChatGPT model performance measures, consider the comparative ratings with state-of-the-art (SOTA) models in Figure 4-4.

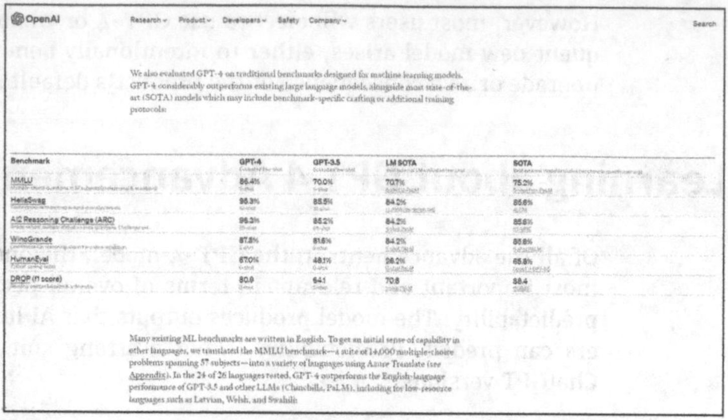

We also evaluated GPT-4 on traditional benchmarks designed for machine learning models. GPT-4 considerably outperforms existing large language models, alongside most state-of-the-art (SOTA) models which may include benchmark-specific crafting or additional training protocols.

Benchmark	GPT-4 Evaluated few-shot	GPT-3.5 Evaluated few-shot	LM SOTA Best external LM evaluated few-shot	SOTA Best external model (includes benchmark-specific training)
MMLU	86.4%	70.0%	70.7%	75.2%
HellaSwag	95.3%	85.5%	84.2%	85.6%
AI2 Reasoning Challenge (ARC)	96.3%	85.2%	84.2%	85.6%
WinoGrande	87.5%	81.6%	84.2%	85.6%
HumanEval	67.0%	48.1%	26.2%	65.8%
DROP (f1 score)	80.9	64.1	70.8	88.4

Many existing ML benchmarks are written in English. To get an initial sense of capability in other languages, we translated the MMLU benchmark—a suite of 14,000 multiple-choice problems spanning 57 subjects—into a variety of languages using Azure Translate (see Appendix). In the 24 of 26 languages tested, GPT-4 outperforms the English-language performance of GPT-3.5 and other LLMs (Chinchilla, PaLM), including for low-resource languages such as Latvian, Welsh, and Swahili.

FIGURE 4-4: Comparison of ChatGPT models using traditional benchmarks provided by OpenAI.

Adjusting to GPT-4's Limitations

GPT-4 also has limitations. It can still hallucinate, that is, deliver information as facts that are not facts and make reasoning errors accordingly. Even so, the frequency of hallucinatory events is greatly decreased. GPT-4 consistently scores 40 percent higher than GPT-3.5 on OpenAI's internal adversarial factuality evaluations (battling AI models that test each other's results; think of it as very fast adversarial fact-checking).

GPT-4 is blind to current events and information, given its data age is cut off at September 2021. In other words, its database is largely comprised of data scraped from the internet up until that date and has not been updated as of this writing. For ChatGPT-4, which is built on GPT-4, to consider recent data or data not available on the internet, you must enter that data in the prompt, use a specialized plug-in such as Wolfram or Zapier, or use the Browsing plug-in to connect ChatGPT-4 to the live internet.

GPT-4 is highly confident in its answers. However, it doesn't always double-check its work for errors, so it can hallucinate (be highly confident of an answer that is provably wrong).

Risks common to all AI models are increased by virtue of GPT-4's increase in scalability — a reference to the sheer size of the database, model parameters, and number of users. However, these risks are known and OpenAI lessens their effect in GPT-4 through the addition of several safety properties and model-level interventions. It can still be manipulated to behave badly, but OpenAI is steadily working to make this much harder to do with each new iteration.

OpenAI uses OpenAI Evals, which is the framework for creating and running benchmarks for evaluating AI models such as GPT-4. OpenAI recently open-sourced this framework to enable crowdsourcing and sharing of benchmarks to produce more reliable AI models through better testing and training.

Users should take care to fact-check outputs by any ChatGPT model. But this extra step isn't so different from checking your own work or someone else's prior to publishing or moving to production, now is it?

As of this writing, OpenAI has not made entering images in the prompt an available option for the public. This feature is currently being tested by select users and developers. There is a developer waitlist for the API in anticipation of a future rollout date.

IN THIS CHAPTER

» Learning about the Responsible AI movement

» Paying attention to OpenAI warnings

» Losing copyright and IP protections

» Reaching for reliability and trust

» Reducing your risks

Chapter **5**

Warnings, Ethics, and Responsible AI

ach model improvement aims to increase stability and overall performance in terms of reliability, accuracy, and ethics. In this chapter, you learn what that means and why the effort is critical.

Making Responsible AI

Almost everyone has an instinctive desire for caution or a sense of foreboding when it comes to AI. A broad industry effort called *Responsible AI* was formed to ensure that AI is responsibly developed by design. This movement is aimed at ensuring that AI models are built on specific principles from the ground up as opposed to having piecemeal measures tacked on after maturity or deployment or — yikes! — disregarded altogether.

Many AI providers and communities embrace the baseline principals promoted by the Responsible AI movement, which include the following:

- >> Accountability
- >> Bias evaluation
- >> Reliability and safety
- >> Fairness and accessibility
- >> Transparency and explainability
- >> Privacy and security

OpenAI, the creator of ChatGPT, has repeatedly stated a commitment to Responsible AI principles. It has also contributed to the movement in a number of ways, including open-sourcing Evals, its framework for evaluating OpenAI models and an open-source registry of benchmarks, and contributing policy research papers.

OpenAI's partners and collaborators also work toward the principles of Responsible AI, but current economic stressors are putting corporate commitments to the test. For example, in line with many recent tech industry layoffs, in March 2023 Microsoft laid off its AI ethics and society team, which was charged with ensuring Responsible AI principles made it into Microsoft products before they ship. Microsoft isn't likely to be the last of the large AI product and services producer to do so.

Troubling developments

Until recently, AI was the domain of a relatively few learned scientists with highly specialized skills. But ChatGPT's explosive arrival on the public scene spurred intense interest across the board. Now it appears that almost everyone is interested in using AI. And quite a few are keen to develop their own; the tools and costs are such that almost anyone can do it.

For example, researchers at Stanford University built Alpaca AI to perform similarly to ChatGPT on several tasks. Alpaca AI was built on an open-source small language model called LLaMA (developed by Meta, formerly known as Facebook). Stanford researchers trained it for less than $600, making it a rough equivalent of a cheap counterfeit copy of ChatGPT.

However, cheap AI can prove to be costly AI. Alpaca AI is very unsafe, in that it frequently produces wrong and toxic responses, and Stanford responded responsibly by yanking it offline shortly after launch. However, the dataset and code for fine-tuning that model is still available on GitHub for anyone to use. The researchers are working on releasing the Alpaca AI model's weights there, too. (Weights rank the importance of various algorithm inputs.) The intention behind making all this accessible is noble: providing a lightweight model for the AI community to study several AI deficiencies in the hopes of making more Responsible AI.

But the nightmare in the story is that anyone can now build an AI model using the dataset and code on GitHub — for about $100 if the processes are optimized, according to Stanford. That's not a far-fetched estimate considering that even cloud computing costs can be reduced or eliminated. We already have multiple reports of people running Alpaca's code on Raspberry Pi computers and Pixel 6 smartphones, thereby skipping any need for cloud computing.

Meanwhile, AI models are popping up in shady communities online too. For example, a week after its launch, the entirety of Meta's LLaMA model was reportedly leaked on 4chan. When it comes to AI, cheaper is far, far worse, at least in terms of safety for humans. For example, an AI model can deliver wrong or harmful information that can physically hurt people if it's acted on, and misinformation can fuel harmful conspiracy theories or spur public unrest. Now think of someone building AI with intentional malice using a model with few to no safeguards. The thought is not comforting.

Don't forget that nation states sometimes have dubious intentions as well. AI of all types is currently in use by most governments, with much of it classified information and therefore unavailable for public scrutiny. Governments worldwide are also concerned about AI being used in terrorist attacks, cyberattacks, or public uprisings.

Concerns over what might be done with AI led to both OpenAI and the Chinese government barring individuals in China from using ChatGPT. But a Chinese company called Baidu has already released its alternative model known in English as Enhanced Representation from kNowledge IntEgration, or Ernie Bot for short.

Ernie Bot differs from ChatGPT-4 in two major ways. Ernie Bot produces multimodal outputs, meaning it generates texts and images, whereas ChatGPT-4 generates only text. And Ernie Bot can't analyze images in prompts but ChatGPT-4 can.

Ernie Bot may differ in safety measures as well. It's hard to tell at this point whether Baidu is working on sufficient safety precautions for Ernie Bot. Everyone is in a big rush to launch their answer to ChatGPT as fast as possible, which isn't good news in terms of ensuring that proper safety and ethical measures are in place and working.

Previously, Baidu released Ernie 3.0, which is largely regarded as a GPT-3 equal. In 2022, it released Ernie-ViLG, which generates images from text prompts. Other ChatGPT-like bots from China-based entities include MOSS, by Fudan University researchers, and Inspo, by a startup called MiniMax.

The US and China have been keenly interested and heavily involved in developing and using AI for years. So have other countries. AI in this context has consequences in both cold and hot wars, world commerce, individual freedom, human rights, and other national, geopolitical, and international policy issues.

Protecting humans from humans using AI

On the flipside, several countries are working to contain consequences from the proliferation of AI models. For example, in December 2022, the European Council of the European Union (EU) proposed a regulation called the Artificial Intelligence Act, which aims to "ensure that artificial intelligence (AI) systems placed on the EU market and used in the Union are safe and respect existing law on fundamental rights and Union values." The US has a new blueprint for an AI Bill of Rights as of October 2022. In the UK, a "Roadmap to an effective AI assurance ecosystem" was published by the Centre for Data Ethics and Innovation in 2021. The World Economic Forum also stepped up with a set of standards and guidelines that it published in 2022 titled "Quantum Computing Governance Principles."

Numerous legitimate integrations of powerful generative AI models like ChatGPT are popping up in existing software almost everywhere. For example, ChatGPT is already in many Microsoft products, from Bing to Office365. GPT-4 APIs can be used to integrate the model with almost any software. Competitive AI models for legitimate uses are also on the rise. One example is Adobe's Firefly tool, which is powered by a generative adversarial network (GAN) AI model.

Understanding the good, the bad, and the ugly

By now you're beginning to realize just how accessible and varied AI truly is! But so are AI providers. How long will they remain interested in responsibly building and retraining AI models when their work can be stolen and counterfeited for mere pennies and in use within a few hours? Now add to that hit on ROI the recent rise in economic pressures to cut costs. Does that mean Responsible AI teams are on the chopping block first?

Where does that leave AI? Where does that leave us?

Even Sam Altman, CEO of OpenAI, has publicly admitted that he's "a little bit scared" of AI. He's also sounding the warning that some AI developers working on ChatGPT-like tools won't apply safety limits. It's just a matter of time until AI models spiral out of control.

Given the huge scale and sweeping capabilities of AI models like GPT-4 and applications such as ChatGPT, it's tantamount that individuals, citizen protection agencies and groups, governments, AI providers, and others join, insist on, or recommit to sustained efforts in containing AI within strong and well-reasoned guardrails designed to protect humans. Costs and corners can't be cut without incurring dire repercussions.

Heeding OpenAI Warnings

OpenAI released each ChatGPT version with clearly posted public warnings. It's essential to heed those. But if you haven't yet read through the opening warning posts or you want to check to see if the warnings have been updated, just ask ChatGPT to list the latest warnings, as I did in Figure 5-1.

Pay special heed to the warning regarding your privacy. ChatGPT is still in training, in all of its models from ChatGPT-3 to ChatGPT-4. This means anything you enter as a prompt (image or text) is likely to be used as training material. Therefore, any of the following conditions may or may not happen:

FIGURE 5-1: ChatGPT-4 lists warnings about its use after prompted.

>> Security is likely not at the same level as is usually afforded to personal identifiable information (PII).

>> Privacy shields, if there are any, may not extend to or follow after any data transfers.

>> Training material may become open-sourced or shared at some point.

>> Your prompts may become a permanent part of training databases for future AI models and therefore almost impossible to ever delete.

>> OpenAI researchers and AI trainers may see your prompts with images and text in their reviews of ChatGPT's performance.

For your own peace of mind, proceed with prompts as though all these situations can be realized.

WARNING

Although all the listed warnings are important, I would single out the incomplete or incorrect information warning. One downside of ChatGPT is that it can be intentionally used to generate highly convincing disinformation and propaganda. I warn you in other chapters but it bears repeating: A more insidious threat is Chat-GPT's capability to hallucinate, or produce responses that sound highly plausible but are totally wrong. In short, don't trust a word that AI says or writes. Double-check everything it outputs.

Considering Copyright and IP Protections

OpenAI has been clear from the start that any text generated by ChatGPT in response to your prompts belongs to you. That's all well and good unless you're trying to copyright it and exclusively use it to make money.

The US Copyright Office ruled that any works containing AI-generated content can be copyrighted only to the extent of human authorship. In other words, whatever part AI writes is not copyright protected by law. If you write the work but use AI-generated images to illustrate it, your words are copyright protected but the images are not. If you reword some of the text that ChatGPT generated, only the words you wrote are protected by copyright. The rest is essentially left in the public domain for anyone else to use.

Lest you think that this is the result of an American quirk or AI bias, consider that the World Intellectual Property Organization (WIPO) reports that most jurisdictions, including Spain and Germany, ruled the same on machine-generated copyright protections decades ago. It remains to be seen if they'll change their minds and consider GPT in general and ChatGPT in particular as original content creators. Right now, the big money is on a resounding "No!"

Publishers and agents worldwide said they were flooded with books, e-books, and other content by people hoping to make quick and easy money on ChatGPT-generated works. Almost none passed editorial muster and no one got a big bag of easy cash. Incidentally, anyone can now copy those works because they are considered fair game.

Further, ChatGPT and other GPT models such as DALL-E may be found guilty of copyright infringement. Copyright-protected works and other protected intellectual property were added to the models' training database when massive amounts of data were indiscriminately scraped from the internet without payment or permission. The potential infringement liability is currently under debate. In addition, because copyright-protected works are in ChatGPT's training database, it may occasionally replicate exact word usage — that is, plagiarize — which could create liability issues for unaware users. A court case may be required to sort out all the legal details.

Keep an eye on rising liability issues, new court actions, and evolving regulations because they may contain emerging threats to your endeavors if you're using ChatGPT or an AI model of similar ilk.

Searching for Predictability

AI can be objectively judged on *predictability*, meaning the percentage of times if delivers the right answer to the same or similar questions. Typically, AI models do not score 100 percent predictability on all questions; rather they have different scores on various types of questions.

But few users rely on actual predictability scoring to determine how much they trust AI. Instead, people are more prone to lean on their perception of AI and their own gut feeling about its responses. In this section, you see how machine tests and human feelings can affect your work with ChatGPT.

Reaching for reliability

In its *GPT-4 Technical Report* OpenAI asserts that GPT-4 scored 19 percentage points higher than the latest GPT-3.5 iteration on OpenAI's internal adversarially designed factuality evaluation. Specific scores in model comparisons are shown in Figure 5-2, which depicts the performance of various ChatGPT models in nine categories.

On public benchmarks such as TruthfulQA, which tests how well the model separates facts from incorrect statements, the base model of GPT-4 scores only slighter better than GPT-3.5. After additional RLHF (reinforcement learning from human feedback) post-training, the GPT-4 model outperformed GPT-3.5 by a wider margin. Counterintuitively, the pretrained model's confidence in its answers generally matched the probability of being correct while the opposite was true of the post-trained model's confidence.

Neither GPT-4 nor GPT-3.5 models have any knowledge of facts and events that occurred after the 2021 cutoff date. These models also do not learn from experience, which can result in gullibility to prompts, reasoning errors, and mistakes that resemble human errors. Biases in the reasoning also exist.

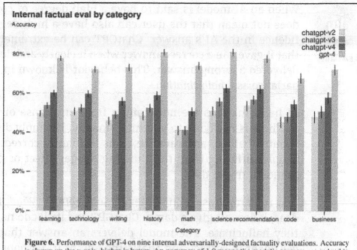

Internal factual eval by category
Accuracy

- chatgpt-v2
- chatgpt-v3
- chatgpt-v4
- gpt-4

Category: learning, technology, writing, history, math, science, recommendation, code, business

Figure 6. Performance of GPT-4 on nine internal adversarially-designed factuality evaluations. Accuracy is shown on the y-axis, higher is better. An accuracy of 1.0 means the model's answers are judged to be in agreement with human ideal responses for all questions in the eval. We compare GPT-4 to three earlier versions of ChatGPT [64] based on GPT-3.5. GPT-4 improves on the latest GPT-3.5 model by 19 percentage points, with significant gains across all topics.

FIGURE 5-2: ChatGPT performance scores in various categories.

WARNING

In short, ChatGPT, regardless of the model used, has a reliability problem. Although this problem has improved over the evolution of models, it's significant enough that outputs should always be fact-checked, especially when ChatGPT content is used for critical functions and decision making.

Readers should always be aware of the inherent unreliability in outputs and not be swayed by the convincing language generated by ChatGPT as reason to skip the verifying step.

Hallucinating versus accuracy

If you read about generative AI models, mention of confident AI or an AI model's level of confidence eventually comes up. In the context of machine learning, *confidence* is a measure of the AI model's estimated probability that its answer (output) is correct based on the information it has (input or prompt).

The four categories used to determine the level of confidence an AI has in its response are repeatability, believability, sufficiency, and adaptability.

When an AI model is said to have a high degree of confidence, it does not mean that the user can also have a high degree of confidence in the AI's answer. ChatGPT can be extremely confident that it gave you a correct answer when it clearly and demonstrably delivered a wrong answer. This behavior is known in AI industry parlance as a *hallucination*.

AI hallucinations are not coming from any sense of malice; the machine is not lying to you intentionally. It simply did the math, spouted babble, and rated itself as brilliantly correct, much like people suffering from the Dunning Kruger effect or delusions of grandeur might do.

And to paraphrase a character in *Gone with the Wind*, frankly, my dear, it doesn't give a damn. ChatGPT and its ilk do not care when they hallucinate. The model delivers an answer that it's highly confident is correct and that's the end of it. Perhaps one day AI researchers will be able to teach AI models to double-check their homework with at least a smidge of humility and to be properly embarrassed when they fail.

When ChatGPT hallucinates, it outputs a convincing bit of nonsense that, if you acted upon it or accepted it unquestionably as true, could prove harmful to you or others. This inaccuracy cloaked in sweet nothings is what researchers are usually referring to when they call a model *unsafe*. The model is not reliably accurate and therefore it is unsafe for you to believe anything it outputs at face value.

As Google puts it, machines learn, but they don't know anything if you equate knowledge with certitude, which is often the case in Western thinking.

ChatGPT works by predicting which words will follow your prompt. It knows nothing. It calculates probabilities and issues an output with the highest probability of being correct, which can turn out to be 100 percent wrong. Do not take this to mean that ChatGPT is a toy or performs a simple calculation. ChatGPT is an astonishing feat of engineering. But it is also flawed.

Does that mean you should consider a flawed ChatGPT or other generative AI model worthless? Absolutely not. Even though its output will have to be consistently and rigorously fact-checked, it can still significantly increase the speed of production. And you can bet your competition is using it or something like it too.

TIP

Think of ChatGPT as a junior assistant that you may need to correct, instruct, and mentor. Despite its shortcomings, this assistant is incredibly fast at bringing you most of what you need to do your own job more easily and quickly.

Humanizing the machine

One of the most remarkable achievements in OpenAI's work in developing ChatGPT and the various models that power it is that this AI model appears human. This development is quite the modern marvel.

Alan Turing, a man of much education and many skills, dubbed his famous Turing Test for AI "an imitation game" wherein a machine could so closely mimic human intelligence and conversation that a human couldn't tell it was a machine. He developed that test in the 1950s and, for much of that time forward, machines fell short. Now several appear to pass the test at least for a while, but they usually get outed eventually.

People generally know that ChatGPT is AI, but users can easily forget that fact as they continue to converse with it. Since the entire interaction from prompt to output is in natural language and flowing at the speed of human conversation, the experience can feel the same as chatting with another human online.

Eventually, ChatGPT makes a misstep that reminds users that this is AI and the jig is up. Even ChatGPT admits that happens in the conversation I had with it on the subject, as captured in Figure 5-3.

Even so, that initial false sense of familiarity breeds trust. And trust is the last thing anyone should place in AI.

Several studies revealed that the human flaw towards humanizing and trusting a machine is persistent. For example, a report titled "Computers in Human Behavior" by researchers hailing from Carnegie Mellon and the University of California Berkeley found that misattribution of blame leads humans to rely on poorly performing AI. In other words, people tend to blame themselves rather than AI for errors. Further, humans continue to wrongly accept the blame, which causes them to "enter a vicious cycle of relying on a poorly performing AI."

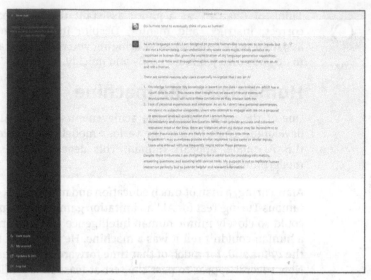

FIGURE 5-3: ChatGPT Plus (premium version built on GPT-4 model) response when asked if people mistake it as human.

Additionally, the researchers found that the user's level of self-confidence, and not their level of confidence in AI, is the deciding factor in whether they accept or reject an AI's suggestions. Their findings point to a need to "effectively calibrate human self-confidence for successful AI-assisted decision-making." In short, humans need to be trained on when to trust themselves and when to trust AI, as opposed to defaulting and demurring to AI.

Human experiences can also color acceptance of the presumed infallibility of AI — especially one that sounds human and benevolent like ChatGPT. People who are cynical and dubious of other people's intent tend to be more skeptical of AI as well. Likewise, people who are more trusting of other people tend to trust AI. But members of both groups have been known to change their minds in response to their personal experiences with AI.

In any case, be aware of human and machine shortcomings and proceed accordingly. Resist your own urge to be friendly and trusting with ChatGPT and its ilk.

As Google's People + AI Research (PAIR) initiative writer David Weinberger put it, uncertainty is seen as a weakness in humans but a strength in AI. Think about that for a minute. Are you making decisions based on misplaced trust in ChatGPT's confidence — or are you going to fact-check it every time?

Mitigating Risks and Liability

OpenAI has gone to significant effort to improve the safety of ChatGPT by continuously improving its alignment with human values and goals. Among the measures they use to accomplish greater safety are feedback from human domain experts for adversarial testing and red-teaming (a group of humans who play an adversarial role in seeking out vulnerabilities), improved safety models (guardrails for the AI model), and a model-assisted safety pipeline that assists by automating machine-learning processes within safety parameters.

Using human experts for adversarial testing and red-teaming, rather than just throwing two opposing AI models in a pit to continuously battle it out and refine each other in the process, is a crucially important move. Domain experts such as cyber-security and international security professionals can find and eliminate or curb risks, such as terrorists using ChatGPT to get assembly instructions for a dirty bomb or a biohacking recipe for a human-engineered pandemic. I'm sure you can see why such intense precautions are necessary.

But other domain experts are also important in refining responses on niche topics, containing offensive remarks, curbing inherent biases, eliminating propaganda and misinformation, and preventing riots and civil unrest.

AI models such as ChatGPT can do lots of good, but when it's allowed to be bad, it can be very, very bad for all of us. Using human experts to deal with the issues and help install the needed guardrails is an absolute necessity.

OpenAI also uses reinforcement learning with human feedback (RLHF) to better match responses to user intent. This approach helps improve the quality of responses. And it helps weed out unsafe and bad behaviors on the part of AI, even if the human user is up to no good, but can also result in the machine becoming overly cautious and not replying even though it's safe to do so.

OpenAI's rule-based reward models (RBRMs) provide additional rewards for the AI model to avoid inappropriate responses and undue caution. The rewards methods, such as when a user clicks thumbs up and thumbs down icons, are indicators that further reinforce which answers are appropriate and desirable and which are not. There are only digital rewards with no donuts or free vacations for ChatGPT in the offering!

As an additional step, OpenAI works with external researchers to improve model performance and safety and to improve their own understanding of potential effects.

But even after all this, some risks remain and the user is well advised to take serious precautions. For example, don't assume that any conversation with ChatGPT or its competitors is or will remain private. See Figure 5-4 for an example of one of the many vulnerabilities AI models like these can have.

FIGURE 5-4: A tweet by Sam Altman, CEO of OpenAI about a ChatGPT data leak.

Potential liability also exists for users who publish unedited Chat-GPT content because ChatGPT and its ilk are known to plagiarize. Copyright and intellectual property rights are not dismissed because a machine infringed upon them instead of a human. Be sure to double-check its work for plagiarism and other issues such as slander before you publish the content.

As to the greater risks to communities, nations, and humanity, a collaborative effort of organizations and government agencies is urgently needed. Otherwise, these rising AI models will quickly get out of hand and undoubtedly create great harm.

Following are steps to take to help mitigate risks and liabilities associated with ChatGPT use:

>> Always fact-check the content it generates.

>> Conduct a human review to ensure that the content is accurate and current.

>> Disclose that you're using AI so readers and reviewers don't feel duped.

>> Check that AI-generated content is compliant with all laws, regulations, and guidelines.

>> Monitor audience feedback and respond quickly if the AI content has created issues.

>> Avoid dependency on AI from yourself or others you work with. You're in charge; AI is just a tool.

>> Use AI responsibly. Never use it to do something morally, ethically, or legally wrong.

These precautions should put you on the right path for mitigating risks and avoiding liability. But in high-risk applications, go beyond even these measures.

Chapter **6**

Probing Professional and Other Uses for ChatGPT

ChatGPT represents a turning point for AI in terms of broad acceptance. As soon as it was available for public use at the whopping cost of free, it became a hit with humans working in a variety of disciplines. But amid the excitement was a touch of unease as workers wondered whether this AI model was the one that would replace them. From fear, excitement, or a mix of both, nearly everyone was eager to see what it could do.

As a result of burgeoning market interest, ChatGPT-fueled applications, look-a-likes, and competitors sprang into being nearly overnight. More than 200 such tools were released in a single week, and the flow of releases hasn't slowed. However, it was clear from the start that OpenAI's ChatGPT and underlying GPT models are the benchmarks for the field.

This chapter covers some of the many uses of ChatGPT for professionals of every stripe and in several disciplines, including but not limited to developers of business and consumer apps. Because

ChatGPT puts programming well within the reach of newbies too, separating its professional and consumer uses is difficult. More uses will come to light over time — and your own imagination may lead you to new uses too.

Finding ChatGPT Embedded in Software

Let's start with a look at where ChatGPT resides in software, tools, and other applications to assist people at work. ChatGPT can be found in the form of extensions and plug-ins as well as embedded or integrated in general work applications and specialized tools. Although GPT is an acronym for Generative Pre-trained Transformer, a type of AI large language model, some people jokingly say it means "general-purpose tool" because of its versatility. You're about to see how versatile and prevalent it really is.

Locating ChatGPT in business software

Given that Microsoft and OpenAI have a close partnership, it should come as no surprise that Microsoft products were among the first to incorporate ChatGPT. For example, Microsoft's Copilot, which is now infused with GPT-4 and called GitHub Copilot X, is essentially ChatGPT fine-tuned for developers. Although Copilot was designed as a developer's tool, its versatility was soon leveraged to create Microsoft 365 Copilot for more generalized use and embedded in Word, Excel, PowerPoint, Outlook, Teams, and other Microsoft applications.

Users will find the embedded AI to be a capable assistant in their daily work. It aids in writing everything from documents to email, builds slides for presentations, and selects and executes formulas in Excel, enabling you to become a power user of these applications with little effort. The point is to make everyone more productive at work, no matter what the nature of their work.

Microsoft's Business Chat goes further by leveraging the AI model to work across Microsoft 365 apps and your data, including your calendar, emails and chats, documents, meeting transcripts, and contact list. Business Chat can also create a knowledge model for your organization by making the data easily accessible to and sharable with others in the organization. This more inclusive knowledge model helps prevent the loss of institutional memory when workers leave the company and take their know-how and knowledge of customers, deals, project status, company history, and other key information with them.

REMEMBER

Always keep data privacy and security in mind. Automated curation of your data by an AI model may expose personal data, proprietary data, and client or customer data that qualifies for PII (personal identifiable information) protections. Microsoft takes data privacy seriously, but it can't protect you or your organization from your own actions. Put strong policies in place to ensure that AI and data are used responsibly.

Microsoft also introduced Dynamics 365 Copilot to include ChatGPT in its CRM and ERP software. This move brings substantial AI support to sales, service, marketing, operations, and supply chain roles.

Microsoft applications are not the only places where you'll find ChatGPT or ChatGPT-inspired AI assistance. Not by a long shot. Here's a small sample of the many types of software that use ChatGPT:

>> **ChatPDF:** Drag and drop a PDF into the app, post a URL, or upload a PDF from your computer, and then add a natural-language prompt to get this ChatGPT adaptation to analyze, summarize, and otherwise help you work with the data in the PDF, be that a book, a scientific paper, a presentation, a slideshow, an article, or other content. The maximum number of pages the app can work with in one sweep is 120. ChatPDF is free and ad-free — at least for now — and you can find it online at www.chatpdf.com. See Figure 6-1 for information on additional features.

>> **Snapchat:** ChatGPT is known as My AI in the Snapchat messenger. My AI is a more limited version than the full ChatGPT model you find online, as far as what it can talk about, and a bit of an experiment for Snapchat. But it's still an interesting application that allows users to chat with coworkers, associates, friends, and family with AI assistance (it can answer chats for you if you're away or too busy to make your own reply). You can also chat directly with My AI to give it instructions or get information.

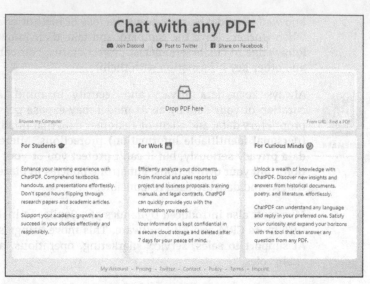

Chat with any PDF

Join Discord • Post to Twitter • Share on Facebook

Drop PDF here

Browse my Computer   From URL Find a PDF

For Students 🎓

Enhance your learning experience with ChatPDF. Comprehend textbooks, handouts, and presentations effortlessly. Don't spend hours flipping through research papers and academic articles.

Support your academic growth and succeed in your studies effectively and responsibly.

For Work 💼

Efficiently analyze your documents. From financial and sales reports to project and business proposals, training manuals, and legal contracts, ChatPDF can quickly provide you with the information you need.

Your information is kept confidential in a secure cloud storage and deleted after 7 days for your peace of mind.

For Curious Minds 💡

Unlock a wealth of knowledge with ChatPDF. Discover new insights and answers from historical documents, poetry, and literature, effortlessly.

ChatPDF can understand any language and reply in your preferred one. Satisfy your curiosity and expand your horizons with the tool that can answer any question from any PDF.

My Account • Pricing • Twitter • Contact • Policy • Terms • Imprint

FIGURE 6-1: Enter your prompt and a PDF to continue to get ChatPDF to work with the info contained in the PDF.

>> **ChatSpot:** HubSpot's integration of ChatGPT, ChatSpot is designed to enable HubSpot users to extract or modify information in its CRM files using only natural-language prompts. This application of ChatGPT will fetch and analyze the customer data you need based on your prompt. Figure 6-2 shows how ChatGPT has essentially become the new user interface for HubSpot, as it has for oodles of other software.

>> **Q-Chat:** ChatGPT is called Q-Chat in Quizlet and serves as a fully adaptive AI tutor, pulling from Quizlet's immense educational content library. This application is mostly for high school and college students, but adults can learn here as well. Q-Chat might be an early glimpse of the future of on-the-job training programs too. You can get a closer look at ChatGPT applications in education in Chapter 7. Figure 6-3 shows Q-Chat tutoring a student learning Spanish.

FIGURE 6-2: ChatGPT is an alternative user interface for HubSpot.

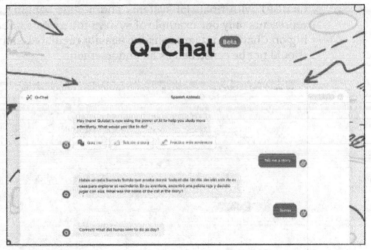

FIGURE 6-3: Q-Chat is an AI tutor that uses ChatGPT and Quizlet's immense educational content library.

ChatGPT is also being integrated in banking and finance applications and other business functions in a variety of software. Examples of where ChatGPT is often integrated in financial technology (FinTech) and business finance applications include customer support, finance AI assistants, investment guidance, economic analyses, and document automation. Integration in existing banking and finance apps is accomplished via the OpenAI API, the official documentation of which can be found at https://platform.openai.com/docs/introduction.

ChatGPT system integrations are also well underway and fast becoming expected by customers. Companies that specialize in system-level integrations, especially for heavily regulated industries such as banking, are appearing on the market or adapting their services just as quickly as app developers are churning out ChatGPT integration with apps. In short, an ecosystem is developing to support ChatGPT applications in heavily regulated industries such as finance and healthcare.

Figure 6-4 is one company's pitch to help banks integrate ChatGPT with financial systems and mobile banking apps. This represents only one example of system integrators already working on ChatGPT integrations for heavily regulated industries and should not be construed as an endorsement.

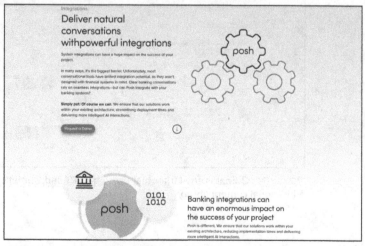

FIGURE 6-4: A company specializing in ChatGPT system integrations for heavily regulated industries such as banking.

As if the proliferation of ChatGPT that I barely touch on in this section isn't enough proof of an exploding adoption rate for an AI model, read on and see where else this new line of generative AI lives.

Integrating with everything, everywhere, all at once

OpenAI began rolling out ChatGPT plug-ins in late March 2023, barely ten days after the public launch date of the GPT-4 model. Plug-ins are specialized tools that help language models like ChatGPT do additional tasks or expand their capabilities, such as using current information from the internet, running specialized computations, or accessing data from third-party services.

The first third-party plug-ins for ChatGPT were Expedia, Fiscal-Note, Instacart, Kayak, Klarna, Milo, OpenTable, Shopify, Slack, Speak, Wolfram, and Zapier. These initial plug-ins were experimental. Others followed as OpenAI approved more developers to build plug-ins.

Plug-ins bolster the usefulness of ChatGPT and add OpenAI's safety measures to the AI's use in these roles. They can also be used to integrate ChatGPT with other software. The effect is far-reaching and market-changing.

For example, Zapier is an automation tool that automates workflows by connecting the apps and services that people use. The Zapier plug-in enables ChatGPT to interact with more than 5000 apps and counting. Meanwhile, Zapier users can use ChatGPT and DALL-E through the integrated plug-in to connect and work across apps more easily. The Zapier page in Figure 6-5 shows ChatGPT and DALL-E connectivity options to automate workflow in and across thousands of apps.

As another example, the plug-in for Wolfram extends ChatGPT's capabilities in mathematical calculations and gives it access to Wolfram's immense library and knowledge base of higher maths, diverse list of formulas, and related mathematical information and theories. With this plug-in, ChatGPT can access real-time and curated knowledge through WolframAlpha and Wolfram Language. Prior to this plug-in, ChatGPT's performance often fell woefully short even on simple math calculations.

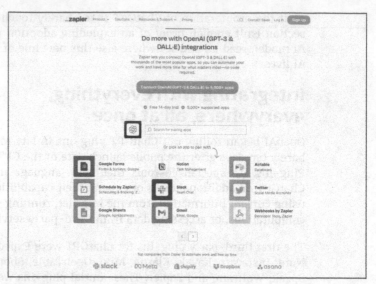

FIGURE 6-5: The integrated Zapier plug-in for ChatGPT enables Zapier users to connect ChatGPT and DALL-E with more than 5000 apps.

Arguably the plug-in that has the biggest effect for the largest number of users is the one for browsing. This plug-in allows the AI model to do research on the internet in real time. An AI model can even decide whether to reach out to the internet for more recent info than its dataset provides. Figure 6-6 shows the ChatGPT browsing plug-in demo, which you can see online at https://openai.com/blog/chatgpt-plugins.

Look for more plug-ins that enable ChatGPT to analyze data not included in its training dataset — such as recent, esoteric, proprietary, and highly personal data — to come soon. You'll find then listed on the OpenAI ChatGPT website and in the pull-down menu on the ChatGPT Plus user interface. Currently, an experimental ChatGPT model, shown in Figure 6-7, makes it possible for ChatGPT to automatically seek out and install whatever plug-ins it needs to best respond to your prompt.

You can expect to find ChatGPT and its ilk nearly everywhere and in every digital form imaginable. It's here to stay, and its AI models will only get stronger and better going forward.

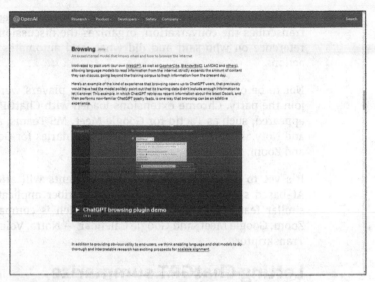

FIGURE 6-6: The OpenAI ChatGPT browsing plug-in demo.

FIGURE 6-7: Plugins Alpha automates the discovery and installation of plug-ins that ChatGPT needs to create the best response.

Zooming in on ChatGPT in virtual meetings

ChatGPT or a version of its underlying AI model quickly appeared in almost every category of software, and virtual meeting software was near the top of the list. Microsoft Teams Premium launched alongside other ChatGPT-embedded Microsoft products. In this manifestation, the AI assistant is called Intelligent Recap, which pretty much explains its role in meetings. It takes meeting notes, transcribes the conversation, organizes the discussion for quick reference on who said and did what, and automates tasks and actions.

Not to be outdone, other virtual meeting players were quick to join the party. Chrome extensions loaded with ChatGPT features appeared, such as Tactiq for Google Meet, MS Teams, and Zoom, and Noty.ai, which delivers ChatGPT summaries for Google Meet and Zoom.

It's yet to be seen how these developments will affect earlier AI-based speech-to-text meeting transcriber applications with similar features, such as Otter.ai — which is compatible with Zoom, Google Meet, and Google Calendar — Notta, Voicegain, and Transkriptor.

Letting ChatGPT summarize and translate

ChatGPT models can understand and translate a multitude of human languages. However, its language outputs are subject to error, especially when the text is complex or the respective vocabularies of the language pairs are widely different. It's always a good idea to have human translators check ChatGPT's work before publishing, broadcasting, or speaking. For help with pronunciation, to practice your language skills, or to learn a new language, check out the ChatGPT plug-in called Speak, which is a foreign language tutor.

ChatGPT also understands many computer programming languages. But the current batch of integrations and plug-ins make ChatGPT most useful in writing computer code. You get to see how that works in a later section, "Coding with ChatGPT and Copilot X."

Leveraging ChatGPT's language versatility is a smart move in many ways. You can paste a sentence or an entire document into ChatGPT and ask it to translate it. ChatGPT can also translate and summarize a document for a quicker read. If you then decide that you want to read the translation of the entire piece, you can prompt ChatGPT to output that as well.

You can also translate text in the same language but in the vocabulary of a different time or writing style. For example, you can prompt ChatGPT to convert text to the style of any writer. Want your manuscript rewritten in Shakespeare's or Hemingway's style? Want it written in the style and language of a writer from another land? Prefer your marketing prose rewritten in the style of your manager or a scientist? Yes, ChatGPT can do any of that. The possibilities are endless.

In Figure 6-8, I randomly pulled ad copy from a marketing email sent to me by Red Lobster and asked ChatGPT to rewrite it as Shakespeare might have written it. The dish sounds yummy to me either way!

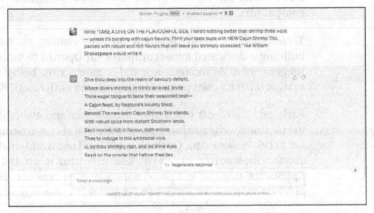

FIGURE 6-8: Red Lobster ad copy as ChatGPT envisions Shakespeare might have written it.

Searching for ChatGPT in other applications

In a matter of a few weeks, ChatGPT and the AI models it was built on rapidly became the backbone of so many applications and services that it was almost impossible to keep track. Speed was of the essence as it became steadily more evident that this hot new technology was no trend but a flame burning down the tools and processes that formerly made work, well, work.

This growing sense of urgency led more than a few competitors to release their own AI models too early. Bard, Google's answer to ChatGPT, is one example. Google was under pressure to respond after Microsoft announced the integration of ChatGPT with its search engine, Bing. The rush to market backfired. Google's parent company Alphabet lost a reported $100 billion in market value in a single day after Bard goofed in a public demonstration and produced an obviously wrong answer to a question.

Both Bard and ChatGPT are works in progress, but ChatGPT was clearly in the lead at the outset. This surprised many because Google has long been thought of as having innovation superpowers and killer AI skills. Bing has long been eating dust from the Google search engine's consumption of market share. It's truly remarkable that ChatGPT turned the tables in favor of Microsoft seemingly overnight. Let that be a lesson in how quickly ChatGPT and its kind can shift or create market advantage for you or your competitors.

To Microsoft's credit, it spent no time resting on its laurels in building a dedicated supercomputer for OpenAI to build and train its generative AI models, nor did it pause after being the first to market with its own product integrations with ChatGPT.

Early on, Microsoft made the Ghostwriter app available to Office users. Ghostwriter is built on ChatGPT and is a writing assistant for Excel, PowerPoint, Outlook, and Word as an add-in. Figure 6-9 shows Ghostwriter in Word. You can find it on the Microsoft AppSource page at `https://appsource.microsoft.com/en-us/product/office/WA200005107?tab=Overview&exp=ubp8`.

FIGURE 6-9: The Ghostwriter add-in for Word.

Microsoft also allowed a select number of ChatGPT-based apps to be added to the Microsoft Store. App stores run by other tech giants have ChatGPT apps too. As Figure 6-10 shows, it's a mistake to think that ChatGPT's integration or repurposed uses are limited to the works of the tech giants.

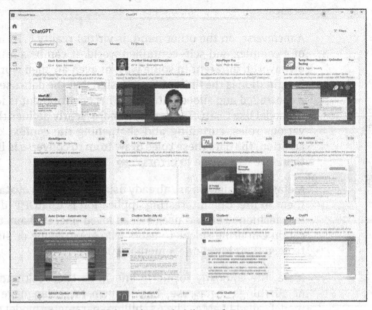

FIGURE 6-10: ChatGPT-based apps in Microsoft Store.

Developers across all industries and company sizes are stepping up to create new ChatGPT-fueled applications. Check app stores and other sources regularly to find new applications for this technology.

Any ChatGPT app could be fake or loaded with malware. Look for apps made or approved by OpenAI, Google, Microsoft, Apple, or some other reputable developer or company.

WARNING

Seeing ChatGPT in AR, VR, and the Metaverse

It didn't take long for creatives of all stripes to turn to ChatGPT to help formulate new ideas. Virtual reality (VR), augmented reality (AR), and metaverse designers were among them.

Augmented reality (AR) applications infuse text, images, and audio atop a view of the real world. The merged presentation of real and virtual is viewed on a screen on, for example, a smartphone, tablet, or smart glasses. Developers are using ChatGPT to rapidly and cheaply create informational text, games, and animated cartoon characters, among other things that they want to overlay on real scenes.

A *metaverse,* on the other hand, is virtual reality (VR) in the form of a complex and self-contained world. It can be a mirror of our own world, different in some way, or even an alien world. Human imagination is the limit of their design, but the data used within is a controlled and siloed database. This environment is ideal for an AI model like ChatGPT because it more clearly defines the model's various roles, curtailing and sharpening the context of each. In addition, the data these roles draw from to converse is limited and therefore less prone to errors.

Metaverse designers are already using ChatGPT in avatars to bring them to life. One interesting application is ChatGPT-driven avatars fashioned after a user's dead loved one. Perhaps that application can bring solace to users who are grieving or simply want to keep their loved one's memory fresh.

Meta, the company formerly known as Facebook and a big fan of all things metaverse, has its own large language chatty AI model called LLaMA. The 65-billion-parameter model was leaked on 4chan about a week after it was announced. LLaMA is not a chatbot but an open-source research package intended for AI researcher use.

It's troublesome that the entire LLaMA package was leaked on 4chan, where many in cybersecurity expect bad people to do bad things with it, such as make more sophisticated spam, phishing attempts, and outright attacks on unsuspecting people in the real world and in metaverses. This may prove to be the case eventually, but the bad guys will need a lot of skill to make it happen because LLaMA is currently in raw form and far from operational.

WARNING

In any case, be aware of the potential threat and tread carefully. Also realize that fake extensions posing as ChatGPT on browsers are a simpler way to fool you than using an AI chatbot to fool you. Watch out for those too.

Discovering ChatGPT in search engines

Search engines were the first place where ChatGPT and competitors showed up, other than in its original browser form. And the first search engine to integrate ChatGPT was Microsoft Bing. One way you can access it is by opening the Bing page (www.bing.com) on your browser. The page shown in Figure 6-11 appears.

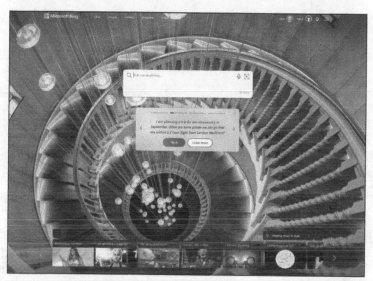

FIGURE 6-11: The Bing and ChatGPT browser page.

 Another way to access Bing is to hover your cursor over the discover icon (shown in the margin) to get to Edge Copilot. You can find the icon at the top right of the sidebar near the search bar.

Google Search uses Bard instead, which is Google's answer to ChatGPT. To access Bard, go to https://bard.google.com by using Google Chrome or another browser. Figure 6-12 shows Bard's prompt page in a browser.

Google is also reportedly creating Magi, a new search engine built on AI to compete with Bing and ChatGPT. Meanwhile, Google is working to beef up Bard and further fine-tune its performance.

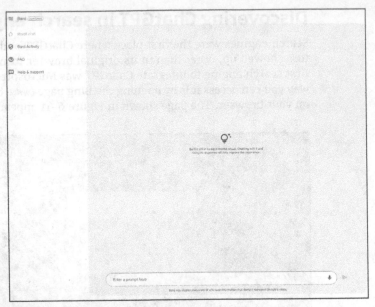

FIGURE 6-12: Bard in the Google Chrome browser.

The Firefox browser enables users to display ChatGPT responses alongside Google Search results through an add-on called ChatGPT for Google, which also, of course, works with Google Search on Chrome. See Figure 6-13. You can find this add-on for Firefox at https://addons.mozilla.org/en-US/firefox/addon/chatgpt-for-google/.

These are three of the most commonly used browsers, so I'll stop here. However, given ChatGPT's astounding proliferation rate, it's safe to say that all browsers will eventually have ChatGPT-like functionality in one way or another.

WARNING

To avoid malware, it's generally safer to use search engines that contain ChatGPT or something similar, such as Bard, than it is to download an extension. However, that's not always true as there are security threats unique to generative AI such as prompt injections. Always use caution in downloading extensions, add-ins, or other apps.

FIGURE 6-13: The Firefox browser extension ChatGPT for Google.

Coding with ChatGPT and Copilot X

Developers are reporting that ChatGPT helps do about 75 percent of their work. They can then focus on more complex parts of the coding work and review what the AI has done before going to production.

Not all developers are happy about the proliferation of ChatGPT and its use in writing code. Their distrust and criticisms are largely warranted. However, for developers who like the new AI assistance, the promise of faster times to production with less effort on more tedious tasks is welcomed. Many look upon such AI-assisted tools as eager and prolific junior developers who need a lot of hand-holding, supervision, and mentoring.

ChatGPT isn't the only or the first assistant-like tool that senior developers are using for help in writing code. The combination of VS Code and Copilot, which now packs more oomph through the Copilot X upgrade, is a favorite for many developers.

VS Code (not to be confused with Visual Studio, an expensive coding software suite) is a free source-code editor. This developer tool for building and debugging web and cloud applications is crazy easy to use. You can find VS Code at `https://github.com/microsoft/vscode`.

Microsoft also makes Copilot, which in this context is a VS Code extension. Copilot looks like autocomplete in that it makes suggestions as you code. To install Copilot, go to `https://marketplace.visualstudio.com/items?itemName=GitHub.copilot`.

Copilot's suggestions show up in gray text on your screen. You press Tab to accept its suggestion and then press Enter to move to the next line. In many cases, Copilot will continue to suggest one line of code after another until you've pretty much written a program. But — and there's always a but, isn't there? — Copilot often makes coding errors. Developers have to watch it closely and edit the machine's work as necessary. Even so, it's amazing how those with no or little experience writing code can use Copilot to write a very simple program.

Microsoft has upgraded Copilot by adding ChatGPT to it and calling the package Copilot X. This substantial upgrade adopts the GPT-4-based model and introduces chat and voice features. Developers out there will be happy to learn that these new features will enable them to make a pull request, summon syntax to help write and execute code on the command line, and request explanations of the code or create full documentations of new or old code. Figure 6-14 illustrates how Copilot X works, starting with monalisa's prompt at the top left.

These tools are not a panacea nor a replacement for human developers. They do, however, signify a giant leap in developer tool enhancements.

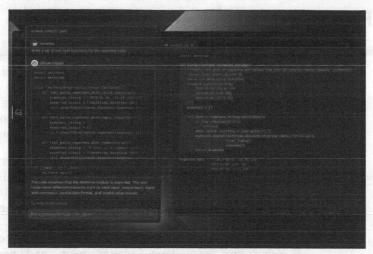

FIGURE 6-14: Copilot X adds ChatGPT for new coding features.

Learning Where to Use ChatGPT for Marketing

The most popular uses of ChatGPT in marketing are content creation and lead generation. Other great uses include sentiment analysis, ad campaign analysis, A/B testing, personalized product and content recommendations, and social media management.

Other types of tools have been available for years to assist with or automate lots of these tasks, and many of them perform very well. However, ChatGPT is unique as a superb and easy-to-use content generator. It also offers a unified approach to marketing tasks and messaging consistency, as well as an advanced means of accomplishing personalized marketing, such as in email campaigns and in making product or service suggestions based on customer preferences and past purchasing behaviors.

Customer service is another area where ChatGPT excels, especially on ecommerce sites. Examples include customer self-service problem resolutions, FAQs, content, and tutorials. ChatGPT is also good at providing support in multiple languages.

Retrieving Smart Answers for HR

ChatGPT can help HR departments with recruitment and hiring efforts by eliminating the need to rely on SEO keywords to sort and screen candidates. Instead, ChatGPT can analyze and summarize a candidate's qualifications based on a resume and other data, comparing that information to the job description and job requirements and providing a better list of matched candidates.

ChatGPT can also assist in other areas of HR where a more humanlike touch is useful and the ease of natural-language communication is more efficient than data entry or limited bot interactions. Examples include onboarding, training, equipment disbursement, security screenings, software access disbursements, employee engagement, vacation and personal time off scheduling, compliance management, and performance management.

Harnessing ChatGPT in Legal

ChatGPT can be used by legal professionals to rapidly write and edit almost all types of legal documents, summarize a document for quick review, and analyze and flag outlier terms in legal documents. It will be a huge help in creating documents and closing agreements in a speedy fashion. Of course, attorneys should always closely review ChatGPT's output before declaring any content it generates as official before executing it.

ChatGPT can also translate esoteric legal language and uncover intentional misdirection in legal documents or communications. For example, lay people will be able to use ChatGPT to summarize everything written or spoken, such as rental agreements, online terms of service, purchase agreements, and SLAs. In this way, ChatGPT will be the bane of existence to legal professionals everywhere.

Discovery is another area where ChatGPT can be a big help to the legal profession. This AI model can make short work of sorting and or summarizing the content of the following:

- **»** Call recordings
- **»** Cell phone carrier records
- **»** Work records
- **»** Visitation records
- **»** Schools records
- **»** Emails, chats, and texts
- **»** Social media posts and images
- **»** Calendar data
- **»** Relationship data
- **»** Sentiment analysis
- **»** Documents and files
- **»** Crime scene and accident scene images and measurements
- **»** Emergency care and healthcare data
- **»** Other items used in discovery to access facts relevant to the case

Just as attorneys once had secretaries to type their documents and missives, only to end up doing it themselves with templates and computer programs, ChatGPT is likely to bring the cycle around to a digital assistant who can handle those tasks automatically and deliver them for an attorney's review incredibly fast.

Tasks that ChatGPT can help with in the legal field include the following:

- **»** Legal research
- **»** Contract review
- **»** Compliance and regulatory analysis
- **»** E-discovery
- **»** Document generation

At some point, you can expect other applications of ChatGPT and GPT models in law, ranging from aiding judges to providing law enforcement with comprehensive information on suspects. But once again, ChatGPT is an assistant or a tool. It's not a replacement for most in the legal and law professions.

Storytelling in Journalism

Now that plug-ins give ChatGPT access to real-time and recent data, it can generate news reports for media outlets on everything from short reports on breaking news and current events to long-form analysis pieces.

However, outside of relatively straightforward fact reporting, ChatGPT is not a replacement for reporters. The reason is simpler than its limitations, shortcomings, and occasional hallucinations.

ChatGPT can't predict a future event with certitude. Nor can it see and analyze hidden events, when the data and evidence is not digitalized, is deliberately obscured, or is labeled incorrectly. Discovery work must be done by human journalists who know where to look for evidence, how to conduct fruitful interviews with often belligerent and uncooperating subjects, and how to pick up on suspicious behaviors such as off-camera body language or other cues that something is amiss.

ChatGPT can analyze a prompt and predict which words come next from data it deems a match. Only humans can conduct an investigation of an event that just occurred in the physical world and is not yet accounted for in digital information. Indeed, much of the data on the internet began as a media or news report. The internet doesn't pull information into itself from thin air and neither does ChatGPT.

ChatGPT can be useful in delivering weather reports and sports scores, but it can't investigate the January 6th attack on the US Congress, chronicle damage in the immediate aftermath of a natural disaster, or catch criminal behavior where data does not exist or is convincingly mislabeled or hidden. These are challenges for human journalists as well, but they are more capable than AI models at figuring these things out and rendering a responsible accounting of events.

Additionally, given that AI hallucinates and presents a danger in spreading misinformation, disinformation, propaganda, and conspiracy theories, it's irresponsible for the news media to allow ChatGPT to report on anything without close and constant supervision. CNET found that out when it trialed ChatGPT to write economic explainers, only for observers to report multiple errors in the copy. ChatGPT could easily kill a news outlet's credibility.

However, ChatGPT is still a helpful tool for journalists. Data journalism, which is data-driven reporting delivered in everything from investigative news reports to lifestyle infographics, has been a goal for news outlets for years, and many do a decent job with it. However, most journalists would rather mind events than mine data. ChatGPT greatly simplifies the task by doing the data analysis and online research for reporters. Again, ChatGPT must be fact-checked, but even so, its time to output far outpaces journalists doing the mundane legwork themselves.

ChatGPT can also help the news media in creating seasonal, evergreen, trending, or custom content, where the data is plentiful and generally not controversial or hurried. Industrious reporters will find more ways to use ChatGPT as a useful tool in a grueling field where words and facts matter.

Consulting ChatGPT in Healthcare

While use cases in healthcare are still emerging and evolving, several are already in the works around the globe.

In medical research, ChatGPT can analyze and quickly summarize large volumes of data from patient records, medical research, medical imaging, and other clinical and research sources. This capability saves time and enables both researchers and clinicians to quickly get the information they need to deliver quality care.

ChatGPT can also conceivably compile and manage patient electronic medical records (EMR) and doctor notes. Telemedicine self-service could be powered by ChatGPT to serve much like insurance nurse lines do now. Patients could tell the bot their symptoms, and the AI model could then triage the level of care needed and deliver instructions when self-care is warranted.

ChatGPT also works well for patient education in everything from generating informative content to answering questions.

Cashing In on ChatGPT in Finance

The initial primary interests of banks and financial institutions in using ChatGPT is in customer service and fraud detection. Other use cases include risk management, investment analysis, compliance and regulation, and more customer-friendly app dashboards.

The finance industry is among the slowest to incorporate new technologies — and ChatGPT and other generative AI models are no exception. And for good reason. If ChatGPT makes errors in banking, the losses to institutions and individuals alike could be substantial.

Chapter 7

Working with ChatGPT in Education

W hen ChatGPT was introduced, students immediately began using it to do their homework. However, many chose to use it not to help with their homework but to do it for them. Educators were not amused. A kerfuffle followed as educators and parents fretted that ChatGPT was an instrument for cheating and would rob students of their ability to hone critical thinking skills. The worriers were only partly right.

Cheaters are going to cheat, and teachers have to catch them if they can. This task is not easy because ChatGPT generates text that is difficult to distinguish from human writing. However, educators are adept at catching cheaters. For decades they've confiscated crib notes, barred calculator use in classes and tests, busted test ringers, checked dutifully for plagiarism, and generally outed the ne'er-do-wells and the ethically impaired. So, really, ChatGPT brings nothing new to this front.

And catching cheaters who use ChatGPT may be easier than catching those who use more traditional tools. For example, you can't catch a cheater who used a calculator unless you see the device because you can't prove a student did wrong by the mere presence of a right answer.

ChatGPT, on the other hand, delivers plenty of wrong answers that can help educators snare wrongdoers. Plus, ChatGPT can be so convincing with its hallucinations that students won't catch on that the answer it gave is incorrect unless they know the correct answer already or look it up to check. It's almost a comical case of cheating gone wrong as learning happens anyway.

ChatGPT also tends to favor and endlessly repeat phrases in its answers. This behavior makes finding cheaters easier because software and professors can look for repetitious phrases in an individual student's assignment and across the homework of many students.

At some point, educators will be able to simply ask an AI model who cheated on a test or an assignment, and it will either confess or point out the evidence. Imagine using a scanner or phone camera to feed into an AI model several classes' worth of assignments. Within minutes, the AI model would grade the assignments, find what each student struggled with in the assignment, offer personalized suggestions, and collar the cheaters too!

In this chapter, I don't spend time on how ChatGPT can be used to cheat because that will get sorted in due time. Instead, this chapter is about how educators can use ChatGPT to better serve their students by offering more personalized support and instruction.

Flipping Critical Thinking to a New Learning Model

As mentioned, some are concerned that students who use AI will miss out on developing critical thinking skills. This problem can be prevented by flipping the teaching model.

Generally, students are taught information and then quizzed. With ChatGPT, the student must ask the right question to unlock the information, an approach that's the reverse of how critical thinking is traditionally taught and tested.

ChatGPT's outputs are only as good as the inputs a human gives it. For students to prompt the AI to deliver the answers they seek, they'll need to think carefully and critically about how to word their query or command first. Teaching students how to think about and write prompts is an effective way to help them develop critical thinking skills.

Consider and compare the following two examples. Figure 7-1 shows a basic prompt and ChatGPT's response.

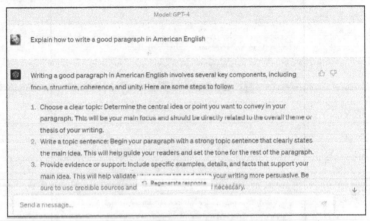

FIGURE 7-1: The prompt here is a basic query, which renders a generic answer from ChatGPT.

Figure 7-2 shows a more thoughtful and strategic prompt, which elicited a more sophisticated and useful response.

This comparison helps illustrate why critical thinking provides a distinct advantage in getting the most out of ChatGPT.

FIGURE 7-2: This prompt is more strategic and asks ChatGPT to provide multiple answers based on various grade and skill levels.

Prompting is so essential to leveraging ChatGPT and other AI models that prompt engineering is a critical skill in the AI field. Teaching students critical thinking skills to use in crafting prompts will ensure that they have a necessary job skill and a bright employment future. Companies will pay big bucks for talented prompt engineers — at least for a while. Eventually, AI models will get better at guessing a user's intention, even if the quality of their prompt is poor. AutoGPT, another emerging AI model, is already capable of making its own prompts from a user's mere suggestion. This improvement will go a long way in making the benefits of AI accessible to everyone, but it won't eliminate the need for creative and critical thinking. In this Age of AI, those who can wield these tools well will prosper, which makes critical thinking skills and prompt engineering excellent job skills for educators to teach — and for educators to learn.

Leveraging ChatGPT to Aid Overworked Educators

Educators are notoriously overworked and underappreciated. ChatGPT can help alleviate at least some of the strain. For example, it can be used to grade assignments and to do so with deeper analysis than educators have time to do. ChatGPT can deliver scores as well as suggestions on where each student is struggling and how the educator can help them in a personalized teaching or mentoring plan.

And ChatGPT can do all this in minutes. Homework, test, and project scores can be computed instantly when students turn them in, or educators and assistants can use AI to score the entire class before the educator heads home at the end of the workday.

ChatGPT can also be useful in quickly developing or adapting lesson plans and completing other work that educators need to do, from ordering supplies to completing tasks required by administrators. Figure 7-3 is an example of how ChatGPT can write lesson plans. Its response was pasted into a Word document to show more of its response here. Responses can be quite lengthy and detailed, but educators can prompt ChatGPT to condense responses if desired.

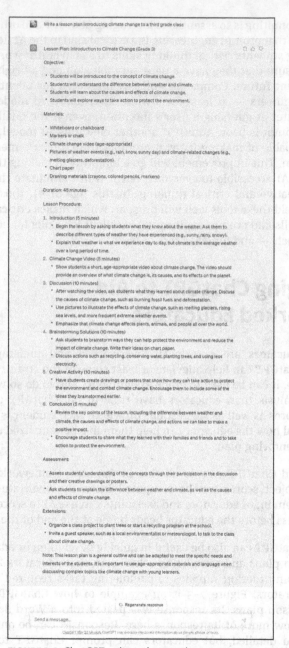

FIGURE 7-3: ChatGPT writes a lesson plan.

Imagine how educators will feel when they get their private time back without any loss in the quality of education they deliver.

Changing How Subjects Are Taught

ChatGPT plug-ins already exist to help students learn. More are on the horizon, and even more are yet to be imagined.

One example is the Speak plug-in for ChatGPT, which is shown in Figure 7-4. The prompt asks ChatGPT to evaluate a student's attempt at translating a question from English to Spanish and to show additional responses in the three most common Spanish dialects. Note that the AI understood the task even with the typo in the prompt.

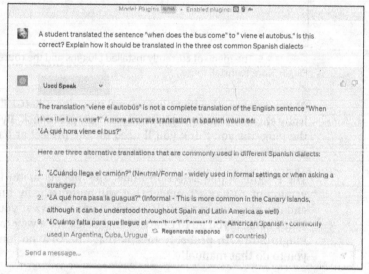

FIGURE 7-4: ChatGPT helps a teacher show a student their mistake in their attempt to translate a question and how the translation can vary depending on regional dialects.

ChatGPT could have attempted this task on its own and would have likely succeeded, but its response is far more accurate with the Speak plug-in. Speak is a specialized foreign-language translation tool whereas ChatGPT is a general language tool, albeit one that can converse in several natural human languages.

I installed Speak from the Plugin Store, which you can access by clicking the down arrow to the right of Plugins at the top right of the ChatGPT user interface, as shown in Figure 7-5.

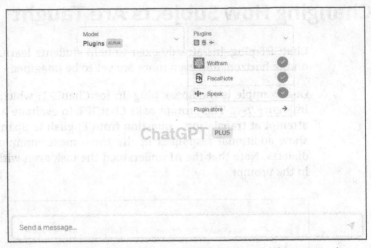

FIGURE 7-5: The menu of currently installed plug-ins and the route to the Plugin Store to install more.

As you can see, I've installed several plug-ins. ChatGPT automatically chooses the appropriate one for any given task. By installing the plug-ins you think you'll need for the project at hand, you'll get better results from your prompts.

The Plugins Alpha selection under the Models menu is an early version of a ChatGPT model that will automatically find, install, and use plug-ins as ChatGPT needs them to answer your prompt. Don't panic if you go to ChatGPT and don't see a way to get to the Plugin Store. In probably means that ChatGPT no longer needs you to do that manually.

Another plug-in example is Duolingo Max, but in this case ChatGPT is being plugged into Duolingo Max instead of the other way around, like the Speak plug-in.

Duolingo Max provides two useful learning tools: Explain My Answer and Roleplay. With a simple tap, foreign language learners can enter a chat with ChatGPT to get an explanation of why their answer was right or wrong as well as further clarification if they want. Figure 7-6 shows an Explain My Answer chat on a mobile phone.

FIGURE 7-6: Duolingo Max's Explain My Answer chat with ChatGPT on a mobile phone.

Roleplay allows Duolingo Max learners to hold real-world practice conversations with ChatGPT. The AI mentors learners on fine-tuning their use of a new language so that they become more fluent and their word choices more natural for different types of encounters and scenarios. Figure 7-7 shows an example of Roleplay on a mobile phone.

Other ChatGPT plug-ins will similarly make existing educational apps more powerful and easier to use. Eventually, AI will become an educator's superapp, meaning a single entity capable of helping educators and students with almost anything.

I'm excited to see how educators will leverage this new tool to reform education and flex their teaching skills to the max in the process. These are indeed exciting times for all!

FIGURE 7-7: A Duolingo Max Roleplay conversation with ChatGPT.

Banning ChatGPT Stifles Education

Banning ChatGPT from schools and education programs is a dire mistake. AI is here to stay and is reshaping the nature of work and, indeed, the human experience.

Educators who do not guide students through this transition are doing them an injustice. Navigating and functioning in the world without AI skills will soon be as difficult as getting by without computer skills and internet access.

The better course is to acknowledge that change really is the only constant and that it's the duty of educators to help students master each new turn. Teach accordingly. Educators are the ones who move a society forward and enable it to adapt.

IN THIS CHAPTER

» **Comparing virtual assistants to ChatGPT**

» **Understanding why keywords are dying**

» **Guarding against misinformation**

» **Grasping what ChatGPT is missing**

Chapter **8**

Using ChatGPT in Daily Life

This chapter introduces you to some of the changes that will ripple through daily life as a result of the ubiquitous adoption of ChatGPT and other generative AI models. At least some of these changes will eventually be noticeable even to people who don't use ChatGPT, don't realize that they do, or have never heard of it.

These are the early days of ChatGPT's appearance on the scene, which means more changes are on the way. This chapter outlines a few of the more foreseeable and likely changes.

Dying Keywords

Search engines introduced keywords to our everyday life. Employees, researchers, and consumers alike learned that if they wanted to find anything in the broad expanse of the internet, they had to figure out which words the search engine could best match to content they wanted it to retrieve.

People adapted their lives to accommodate keywords in their personal sphere of existence as well. For example, resume formats and job applications changed, with distilled content and added keywords so a machine could search, sort, and rate candidates. One downside of this practice is that some candidates could be the most qualified and still not be considered for the position for want of the right keywords. On the flipside, companies looking to hire could miss great job candidates because of poorly written job descriptions and requirements that resulted in a collection of poor performing keywords that applicants might not think to use.

Yet keywords have persisted because they are useful overall. Beyond sorting lots of resumes and job applications quickly, keywords help companies with important tasks ranging from research and fact-checking to better-targeted marketing campaigns.

The latter birthed the search engine optimization (SEO) industry. *SEO* is a process that largely depends on the strategic use of keywords to improve the quality and quantity of unpaid traffic to a website or web page. But keywords are also used to match advertising to online consumers in paid advertising.

There are more examples of how keywords became essential and prevalent, of course. But for our purposes, you can think of SEO as being a routine and important element in our daily lives.

Then along came ChatGPT to upend the keyword and SEO cart. Broadly speaking, ChatGPT works by predicting the words that will follow the words you used in your prompt. That's why writing great prompts is so critical to getting great results.

Generative AI models like ChatGPT do not use keywords to work. Instead, they rely on complex calculations of word context and meaning plus user intent. Sometimes ChatGPT gets that right, and sometimes not, but either way it does so with no regard for our heretofore crucial keywords. As a result, keywords and SEO are dying.

It won't be a quick death because mankind has just begun the transition from heavy reliance on search engines to dependence on generative AI. The full transition will take time, but even so, some will likely hold on to search engine use for a variety of reasons. One important reason is to have a way to fact-check Chat-GPT outputs. This task might require users to discover search engines other than Google, Bing, Yahoo!, Baidu, and DuckDuckGo if the big search engines pivot more towards generative AI than keyword-based search.

Right now, some search engines are integrating generative AI but keeping the emphasis on search. Examples include Microsoft's Bing Chat and Google's Bard.

However, if users shift in large numbers towards generative AI chatbots and away from traditional search, the search engines will make a more pronounced shift too. And that scenario is highly likely just as a matter of user convenience. It becomes increasingly likely if generative AI becomes better controlled, meaning that it no longer frequently hallucinates (convincingly lies).

Perhaps search engines will adapt and use search functions to provide instant fact-checking alongside chat results to add user value and protect their own investments. Perhaps they'll take a different course.

Meanwhile, ChatGPT is also actively integrating search engines via plug-ins. One example is WolframAlpha, a knowledge engine specializing in complex mathematics. Figure 8-1 shows the WolframAlpha user interface with a reference to its availability through ChatGPT Plus, the premium version of ChatGPT. Another is Expedia, a search engine specializing in travel options and deals.

If ChatGPT holds this course, it could become a superapp, having incorporated a lot of other apps, many of which are specialized search engines. It's a safe bet that ChatGPT can predict better keywords for the various search engines than you and I can. The quality of ChatGPT results using specialized plug-ins should be stellar.

Time will tell how search engines and generative AI such as ChatGPT coexist, or whether one consumes the other. But in any case, the days of keywords and SEO are clearly numbered.

Moving from Information Search to Knowledge Assistants

Almost everyone is familiar with and uses a virtual assistant such as Siri, Alexa, Google Assistant, or Cortana. Up until the advent of ChatGPT and its ilk, virtual assistants used a different form of AI coupled with automated and keyword-based search. Although the algorithms also consider other inputs, such as your location, past purchases, and personal preferences, virtual assistants primarily run on search engines.

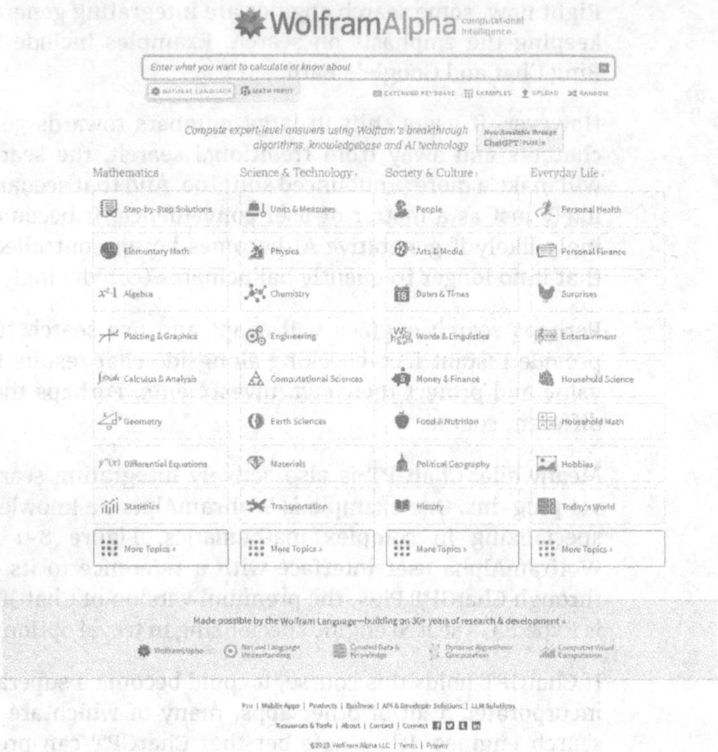

FIGURE 8-1: The WolframAlpha user interface with an option that makes it accessible through ChatGPT Plus.

That situation is beginning to change. For example, Cortana, Microsoft's virtual assistant, uses the Bing search engine, which is now integrated with ChatGPT. Meanwhile, Google Assistant, which is tied to Google Search, can benefit from integration with Google's Bard. These virtual assistants, however, may be replaced with next generation ChatGPT-like versions. You see where all of this is going, right?

Take a look at Figure 8-1, which shows a comparison between Google Assistant's response and ChatGPT's response to the same user question.

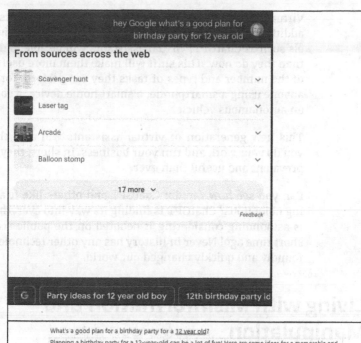

FIGURE 8-2: Google Assistant delivering search results versus ChatGPT delivering AI response.

Virtual assistants are becoming knowledge assistants. With the addition of or replacement by more powerful generative AI models such as ChatGPT, virtual assistants will be able to do far more than they do now. This shift will make them more useful in terms of the number and types of tasks they can perform for just about anyone using a smartphone, a smart home device, a computer, or an autonomous vehicle.

This new generation of virtual assistants will also change how you do your work and run your business. In short, they'll be more prevalent and useful than ever.

Can you see how rapidly ChatGPT and others like it are becoming ubiquitous? ChatGPT is finding its way into everything, which is astounding considering it debuted on the public scene such a short time ago! Never in history has any other technology so profoundly and quickly changed our world.

Living with Misinformation and Manipulation

ChatGPT and other generative AI models are subject to errors, chief among them being hallucinations, which is AI parlance for the machine being convinced it's correct when its answers are glaringly and indisputably wrong. In addition, human biases end up unintentionally transferred to AI models. These are reasons enough to be careful about accepting AI outputs at face value.

But everyone should also be aware that AI models can be trained to deliberately spiel propaganda, misinformation, conspiracy theories, manipulative language for a hidden agenda, biased information, security attacks, and outright cons.

In short, it's more important than ever to teach the citizenry of every country how to discern factual information from incorrect, manipulative, or malevolent narratives. Do not mistake an AI model's chatty friendliness with it actually being a friend. It isn't. It's not a person. It's a tool used by people, and as such it's subject to all sorts of mischief as well as helpfulness. I can't stress enough why everyone needs to fact-check everything ChatGPT generates.

Also, be aware that there isn't just one of any given AI model. Any one model brings about many of its kind. Some are the same at the base but trained differently, making them whole nother animals, as we say in the South. Others are augmented, as Microsoft says it has done to ChatGPT to make Bing Chat.

You get the picture, now finish the thought: Just because one ChatGPT model or use case proved trustworthy doesn't mean they all are by extension.

Some versions of ChatGPT and the like have better guardrails than others, but users can't see them so you're not going to know for sure that they're there. Be careful.

Further still, even AI scientists don't know exactly how AI "thinks," meaning how it arrives at its answers. That's why the industry is working so hard to develop Explainable AI. We need AI to tell us how it came to each conclusion so that mere humans can better judge and, we hope, control what it does.

Keep all this in mind while working with ChatGPT and its kind. It may feel like you're having a private and safe conversation with something very humanlike, but ChatGPT is both more and less than that. Stay detached and logical while using these models. And always, always check its homework.

Narrowing Options

Unfortunately, along with convenience comes a narrowing of options. For example, a convenience store carries fewer brands and fewer options on its shelves to increase shopper convenience. You park at the door of a smaller store, run in, grab your stuff, pay more than you would in a big-box bargain store, and off you go. Super convenient but at a price. Think of ChatGPT as a convenience store offering a one-stop shopping experience for the internet and apps.

You drop by, type or voice your prompt, get a response, and you're on your way. Its fast, unified responses are convenient compared to the process of thinking which keywords to use, entering them in a search bar, reading through the list the search engine produces, weeding out the ads, and finally selecting a source so you can read all that content and maybe find what you're seeking. If you don't find it, you must repeat the process. Compared to the ChatGPT experience, search is a lumbering, exhausting, and frustrating ordeal.

Many users are going to opt for ChatGPT based on convenience. But that convenience comes at an extra, albeit not immediately noticeable, price.

Did you see any sources listed so you know where ChatGPT got its information? No? Hmmm. Can you tell whether ChatGPT used a single source or several sources in generating its analysis? Hmmm. Do you see anything indicating whether the information ChatGPT gave you is current? Ah. You forgot about OpenAI's warning that ChatGPT's database is two years old, didn't you? Uh-huh. We all do that sometimes.

Never fear, several plug-ins and integrations are now giving ChatGPT access to the live internet! Yay! Er, no. Go back over the questions we just covered. Can you see any information — sources, dates, cross-references, and other data or metadata qualifying ChatGPT's response — in the machine's narratives now that ChatGPT can be connected to the internet? No. That information is still not there.

A search engine gives you all of that vital information by providing links directly to its sources. Using ChatGPT information without these insights may be more convenient, but the price of the consequences may prove to be far more than you expected.

As you review ChatGPT outputs, keep in mind that you may be looking at an answer that is too narrow to be appropriate in your work or life. One unknown source and one perspective — as well as the repetitive phrasing and answers that ChatGPT tends to favor — are influencing how you think and act. Are you okay with that?

Use ChatGPT as the great tool that it is, but don't let it think for you!

Chapter **9**

Recognizing the Ways ChatGPT and Generative AI Will Change the World

hatGPT is a global phenomenon that sparks fear and excitement worldwide. Because it sounds human but is made of advanced AI software connected to an internet-sized database, people assume that it's better — or worse — than humans.

Reactions run the gamut. Maybe this AI is the first machine over-lord of sci-fi lore. Maybe it will save mankind. Perhaps it will take all our jobs and eliminate our purpose for living. Maybe it will make everything cheap and banish inflation.

But ChatGPT is only a mindless tool. It's as good or as bad as its users' prompts — notwithstanding a scary or offensive machine rant or hallucination or two.

Understanding What Is and Isn't of Real Concern

To give ChatGPT's seemingly sudden appearance in the world some much-needed perspective, think back to past cycles when a new technology was assumed to be the end of a previous one. The advent of radio was going to eradicate newspapers. TV was thought to be a radio slayer. And the internet was supposed to be the TV killer. But that's not what happened. Although these forms of communication have changed over the years, they all co-exist.

ChatGPT is yet another communication medium. It generates narratives in a conversational format. But just like the communication media that came earlier — newspaper, radio, TV, and the internet — ChatGPT isn't going to replace much that came before. It certainly isn't going to replace search engines. Each serves a distinct purpose the other can't recreate — although at some point, the two technologies might converge.

ChatGPT isn't going to replace people in their jobs, either. Rather, it will eliminate some jobs and create others. This is a cycle you've seen more than once. For example, both the invention of the assembly line and modern-day automation replaced some workers but also created jobs. ChatGPT will eventually spark a similar job cycle.

ChatGPT is a powerful tool that can assist humans in doing many different kinds of work. And when its use is coupled with something capable of a physical manifestation, such as 3D printers or automated physical infrastructure, the effect in the real world can be astonishing. Workers who become adept at using it to increase their own productivity and creativity will be best positioned to advance in their existing careers or move to new ones.

Measuring the Good and Bad in ChatGPT

If what I've written so far seems reassuring, you're mistaken. ChatGPT is an existential technology, a hard pivot in human experience, and a doorway to a far different kind of future. It's the harbinger of the AI Age and a pronounced mark of the arrival of the Fourth Industrial Revolution. If that terrifies you, you're still mistaken.

Humankind, not software, is equal parts scary and saintly. AI in its current forms mostly mirrors that duality. ChatGPT certainly does.

The most threatening aspect of ChatGPT is its capability to rapidly create and spread harmful disinformation in every aspect of human life, from politics to healthcare and everything in-between. It can lie, hallucinate, misinform, and make stuff up. How human of it.

The most endearing aspect is its capability to help people create things that do not yet exist. ChatGPT can help authors and scriptwriters create stories, filmmakers make incredible special effects and new films on the tiniest of budgets, performance artists consider new routines, musicians create new scores, architects design new kinds of buildings, and photographers capture realistic images of decidedly unreal subjects. No aspect of human creativity is beyond the scope of ChatGPT's enhancement and collaborative capabilities.

Weighing Job Threats and Other ChatGPT Liabilities

Can ChatGPT be used to outright replace the work of creative people? Yes, it can. Note that publishers' inboxes and self-publishing platforms are already filled to the brim with ChatGPT-generated books. But also note that most of them are truly awful reads.

The people who jumped to create works using only ChatGPT were driven by greed, not by any desire to create true art. It takes a true artist to shape a prompt for ChatGPT that will render a magnificently original creative work.

The lack of quality coupled with recent events in the US that deny copyright protection of such works — while enforcing copyright protections for any plagiarism ChatGPT and its ilk use in the creation of such works — will soon rob the greedy of their dreams of easy wealth.

And like the content farms of yesteryear that tried to game search engines by producing godawful reads full of keywords, those using ChatGPT to create fast content for cash will soon fall into obscurity.

But do remember that the fatal fall for content farms came from human hands, in spite of the intense efforts at search engine optimization (SEO). Specifically, owners of search engines didn't want to render lists of trash results to users, so they drove the work of content farms to the far outer corners of the search universe. Mainstream media, seemingly on its last leg and hemorrhaging badly, began to rebound almost immediately.

We'll likely see that pattern again with ChatGPT content. Human artists and experts will continue to thrive, with ChatGPT taking a permanent place as an important tool in their toolbox.

The same will likely hold true for most knowledge workers. Using ChatGPT in place of or without the direct supervision of workers who possess the necessary knowledge will prove to be a horrendous and expensive mistake. Such careless reliance on ChatGPT alone will also open companies to a slew of liabilities while producing little in the way of efficiencies or revenue.

Sampling the Disruptions Ahead

That said, it's time to look at the ways ChatGPT and its generative AI ilk are likely to further disrupt our world:

>> **Public trust will be further eroded.** Generative AI can produce fake voice tracts that are identical to the original voice, provide tons of disinformation on nearly every subject, and manipulate human behavior through carefully formed narratives. It will be much harder for citizens in any country to discern reality from deception and truth from untruth. Even the results of fact-checking will be suspicious given that generative AI can mimic trustworthy sources. Security teams will be pushed to the limit to keep pace. Fortunately, AI models can be trained to help spot and stop these threats. Unfortunately, it'll take much longer to rebuild public trust.

>> **The rise of superapps will begin.** Until this point, apps were embedded with AI to make them faster and better at performing tasks requiring immense amounts of information. But ChatGPT can be considered a superapp in that it can do tasks that formerly required several separate apps, and it can do so by automatically selecting plug-ins to augment its own performance as needed.

>> **ChatGPT integrations will eventually be replaced with connected AI.** Chat GPT is being integrated with search engines, apps, and other technologies that may or may not have other AI embedded or integrated. Soon, various forms of AI will be connected directly rather than indirectly through app integrations. Some think this is the path to the infamous singularity, while others see it as little different than integrating multiple apps.

>> **Smart automation will become more intelligent and versatile.** Smart homes, smartphones, smart TVs, smart things of all kinds will become more helpful as virtual assistants like Siri and Alexa become supercharged with generative AI capable of understanding and even anticipating user needs.

>> **Knowledge work will be augmented.** Workers will spend less time handling mundane functions in knowledge work and more time focused on creating more knowledge. For example, data analysts can use ChatGPT to do the needed analysis as well as write final reports. This will free data analysts to look deeper into the data for more refined insights and to unearth knowledge that may have been missed earlier. Likewise, lawyers can use ChatGPT to write legal briefs, contracts, and other legal documents. The signers can use ChatGPT to condense all the legal forms into an easy-to-understand summary. Opposing attorneys can do likewise, and thus free their time to develop a strategy to counter any challenges or sticking points that ChatGPT uncovers in evidence or legal agreements.

>> **Marketers and advertisers will produce more content in a continuous delivery cycle.** Because companies seek to stay ahead of emerging trends and be the first-to-market on new ideas, marketers and advertisers will use ChatGPT and its siblings to produce content and ads extremely fast to sell in the moment. As the product changes with the moment, so too will the ads.

>> **Education will be disrupted.** Long teetering on obsolescence, education as we know it will be disrupted by ChatGPT and generative AI of all forms. The nine-month education model designed to let farmer's children out of school for planting and harvesting is no longer needed or useful. Neither is the mass conveyor-belt-like grade system or formalized testing. ChatGPT will enable educators to move

to more customized learning models wherein students progress according to their competency with the subject rather than their age, school grade, or time spent on the subject matter. How can it do that? By enabling educators to analyze each student's data and create a customized learning plan for each student. Homework, tests, and other measures of subject competence can also be assessed and reported by generative AI.

>> **Media will use ChatGPT to break news faster.** ChatGPT can't do investigative reporting. That task requires human reporters to find hidden information and conduct interviews. However, ChatGPT can help fill in the background info for color and context and get the final piece to audiences faster. Journalists will be valued more for their ability to dig up or create additional insights rather than for simply reporting existing and often easily found facts.

>> **Customer service will become far more personalized and instantaneous.** ChatGPT can discuss issues with customers, offer solutions, give instructions in product support, facilitate returns that fit the customer's circumstances, and resolve issues faster and with less friction than typical customer service processes. For example, instead of a shopper searching a company's website for a given product, ChatGPT can become a personal shopper and deliver product selections that fit the taste, size, and style preferences of each individual shopper.

>> **Healthcare will improve.** ChatGPT can provide doctors with information from the latest research and recommendations based on the probability of success for a specific patient. ChatGPT can act as a physician's assistant in other ways too. In addition, ChatGPT can save lives by providing information for laypeople to help them prevent health issues, deliver emergency treatment, and accurately assess whether a doctor's attention is warranted.

ChatGPT and generative AI will change our daily lives and future human experience in many more ways than this already long list, though not all of them can be foreseen.

Chapter **10**

Ten Other Generative AI Tools to Try

ChatGPT is a global phenomenon, but it is not without peers. In this chapter, you look at ten other generative AI tools that contribute to the advancement of AI and natural-language processing. Each is unique in terms of strengths and weaknesses, and in features and capabilities. You might find that a different model, one made by OpenAI or another company, would be more useful for a given project or a better fit with your preferences. Because more alternatives are coming, it's worthwhile to look around periodically to make sure you're using the generative AI model that bests fits your needs.

The suggestions in this chapter are not meant to discount the incredible breakthrough that ChatGPT represents, the hard pivot in human acceptance of AI that its release marked, nor its role as a harbinger of existential change. Any interpretation of ChatGPT as a simple word-pattern prediction tool is a gross underestimation of the notable human achievements required to make it and the powerful nature of the tool itself.

DALL-E and DALL-E 2

DALL-E and DALL-E 2 are ChatGPT siblings. These models generate computer images described by users in text and images entered as a prompt. The user doesn't need to be skilled in photography or other visual arts. However, renderings from a professional artist will be far more sophisticated because their prompts are. Note that AI-generated images are not currently protected by copyright in the US and several other countries.

DALL-E is a 12-billion parameter version of GPT-3 that generates images rather than text. DALL-E 2 is an optimized version that generates more realistic images with a greater degree of accuracy and four times the resolution. Which you use is often a matter of personal preference and your requirements. For example, a lower resolution is usually preferred for images and icons on web pages whereas a higher resolution is required for large photo prints and metaverse renderings.

To use DALL-E, go to https://labs.openai.com. The page shown in Figure 10-1 appears. For DALL-E 2, go to https://openai.com/product/dall-e-2. If you've already set up an OpenAI account to use ChatGPT, you can begin to use DALL-E or DALL-E 2 immediately. If you haven't yet used ChatGPT, go to the same link for DALL-E or DALL-E 2 and follow the prompts to set up a free OpenAI account, which then gives you access to ChatGPT and DALL-E or DALL-E 2.

The instructions to use DALL-E and DALL-E 2 are similar, so if you can use one you can easily use the other. To use DALL-E, enter your text prompt or upload an image you want to edit.

Image archive

Share your images

Purchase credits, outpaint, and more

Enter prompt

Upload an image

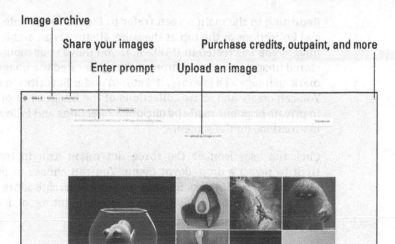

FIGURE 10-1: DALL-E main screen.

DALL-E has advanced editing capabilities. For example, you can prompt it to add elements in the same style and background as the image to create a new image or tell a bigger story. It can also *outpaint*, or extend an image beyond its borders, by analyzing the overall image and using cues such as the paint colors on the edges of the image. For a wonderful timelapse depiction of the outpainting process on the famous *Girl with a Pearl Earring* by Johannes Vermeer, shown in Figure 10-2, visit the OpenAI blog post at https://openai.com/blog/dall-e-introducing-outpainting?utm_source=tldrnewsletter.

Credit: Girl with a Pearl Earring by Johannes Vermeer. Outpainting created by August Kamp × DALL·E
FIGURE 10-2: *DALL-E used to extend* Girl with a Pearl Earring.

Returning to the main screen (refer to Figure 10-1), note History and Collections at the top of the page. History is an archive of the images you've created in DALL-E. If you move your mouse over a stored image, you see the prompt that generated the image. If you mark an image as a favorite, it's stored under Favorites in History. You can create and share collections of the images you prompted in private or public mode by clicking Collections and following the instructions on the screen.

Click the user icon or the three-dot menu icon in the upper right to reveal a drop-down menu. You can choose to purchase credits (115 credits cost $15 US) so you can create more images than allowed in the preview or trial, try outpainting, or access the OpenAI API.

DeepL Write and DeepL Translator

DeepL Write is a tool to improve your writing rather than answer general and broader questions. This language model is more specialized than ChatGPT and therefore has more limited and focused uses.

To try out DeepL Write, go to www.deepl.com/write. DeepL Write is in beta and still learning, so it's free at least while users are helping to train the model.

You enter text in the left panel, shown in Figure 10-3. Then in the right panel, this AI model shows you how to improve or rephrase your text. DeepL Write captures context, nuances, and style in your original text and uses that to generate rephrasing suggestions and word alternatives.

If you click the speaker icon, DeepL Write converts the text to speech and reads it back to you. Reading text aloud is an age-old writer test to ensure that the text flows smoothly and naturally. This is a nice touch for improving your writing or your ability to pronounce words correctly, especially in a language that isn't your mother tongue.

DeepL Translator is a downloadable app and also available as a browser extension. It enables you to translate languages in any computer application or document. You can translate up to 5,000 characters (not words) for free. If you upgrade to one of the

premium versions, you'll get an unlimited number of translations, expanded file upload limits, and additional features. Premium versions range from $8.74 per user per month to $57.49
per user per month. All premium plans require an annual payment. Note that you don't have to log in to use the free version.

Speaker icon   Your text here   DeepL Write's response here

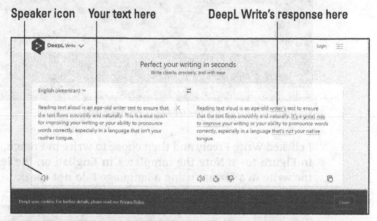

FIGURE 10-3: DeepL Write waiting for you to enter text.

DeepL Translator and DeepL Write are operated by DeepL SE in
Cologne, Germany. Since the company is located in the EU, users
enjoy far greater privacy and confidentiality protections than
those offered by AI companies in some other countries, such as
the US. Even so, be cautious about sharing sensitive information
on this or any other AI application.

Cedille

Cedille is an open-source French language model based on GPT-J,
a different GPT model than the ones we've discussed so far, which
was developed by the EleutherAI team. You can find it at https://
cedille.ai/. And yes, you can use it even if you don't understand
a word of French. Language-based AI models are helpful like that!

After you access the website, click the Try It for Free button and
off you go! Figure 10-4 shows the simple task buttons you can
select to generate the text you need.

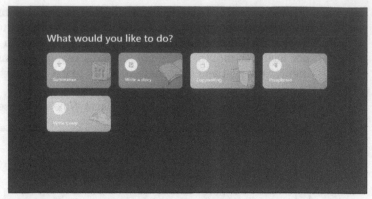

FIGURE 10-4: Accessing the free version of Cedille.

I clicked Write Freely and then chose to write in French, as shown in Figure 10-5. Note the templates in English on the left to help me write in a format using a language I do not speak.

FIGURE 10-5: The Cedille Free Writing prompt page.

If you want more than a sample of what this model can do, you'll need to upgrade to a premium plan. Prices range from 9€ per user per month, or about $10 in US dollars, to 139€ per user per month, or about $152 depending on the current euro-to-dollar conversion rate.

Notion AI

Notion AI is a productivity and note-taking app built on ChatGPT and developed by Notion Labs. Notion is touted as an app that organizes all your work into one app.

For $10 per month per user, you can use the Notion AI writing assistant to automate lots of language-based tasks. Organize notes, extract bullet points or summaries from long documents, make changes to documents, respond to emails, craft marketing messaging, and perform other language-intensive tasks. If you're using the Notion app already, you can highlight text in another document or use a keyboard command to summon Notion AI to do your bidding without opening the Notion app.

Unlike other models mentioned in this chapter, Notion AI is not trained by users. The data you enter in prompts and the machine-generated narratives you use in part or in whole in other apps are private and encrypted. The only data the company says it shares with partners is data necessary to provide features to their own customers.

To check it out, go to www.notion.so/product/ai. As Figure 10-6 shows, handy drop-down menus make variations on prompting fast. Think of Notion AI as a capable text editor on the fly!

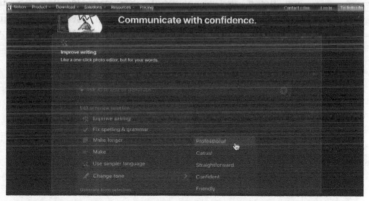

FIGURE 10-6: Drop-down menus let you quickly edit Notion AI's responses.

YouChat

You.com (https://you.com) is an AI-powered personalized and privacy-based search engine with YouChat, similar to ChatGPT, as its chat function. You.com users personalize this search engine by voting up or down on results, result sources, and apps. This fine-tunes the search engine to deliver search results according to the user's preferences.

The privacy afforded by this search engine is similar to Duck-DuckGo in that advertisers and ad providers such as Google can't see or use your search history and other data. You.com also doesn't show you targeted ads based on your search or results voting.

YouChat is based on OpenAI's ChatGPT but has a strong competitive edge in a couple ways:

» It cites the sources for the info it includes in its responses.

» It's connected to the internet so it can use Google sources, something other AI chatbots can't do because they don't have internet access.

To try out YouChat, go to https://you.com/search?q=who+are+you&tbm=youchat&cfr=chat. In Figure 10-7, note the options above the prompt field, which enable you to search images, videos, news, and social media. You can also use the Maps option, which is Google Maps but Google can't see who you are. YouChat has access to more data than some ChatGPT model adaptations because it's connected to the internet.

FIGURE 10-7: YouChat and ChatGPT prompt in similar ways.

If you want to work directly with You.Com AI models to perform other tasks such as YouChat, YouCode, YouWrite, and YouImagine, go to https://you.com/ and select from those options, as shown in Figure 10-8. The More option takes you to the search engine options should you want to conduct an internet search.

FIGURE 10-8: You.com AI options for chatting, coding, writing, and creating images.

ChatSonic

ChatSonic is another Google-supported model, so it's connected to the internet and has access to current information. The voice prompting and AI image-generation features are a major plus for content creators. ChatSonic is like ChatGPT and DALL-E rolled into one.

To create an account and access ChatSonic, go to https://app.writesonic.com/signup?feature=chatsonic. Next, set the permissions to customize ChatSonic's performance, as shown in Figure 10-9.

After you complete the setup, you see the ChatSonic interface shown in Figure 10-10, where you have access to a prompt library and more than a hundred features.

ChatSonic is ideal for those who want to create content quickly and with as little effort as possible. However, it can't do math, so you'll have to calculate how much you're willing to spend for this level of instant gratification from an AI-powered content mill. After the free trial, monthly costs range from $12 to $650 per month, depending on the number of words you use. Click the Upgrade button to see pricing options.

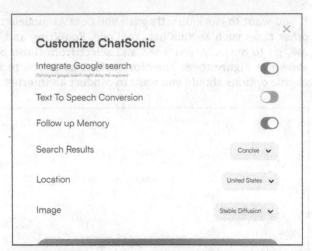

FIGURE 10-9: ChatSonic is customizable at setup and while you're using it too.

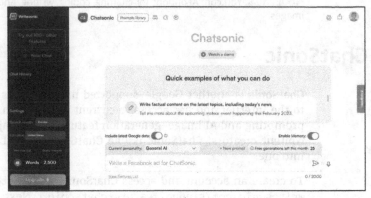

FIGURE 10-10: ChatSonic's prompt page.

Poe

Quora, a social question-and-answer website and knowledge platform, developed Poe, which is an AI chatbot platform. Think of Poe not as a chatbot but as a place where several AI model-based chatbots can coexist so that Quora users can interact with any of them at will. Among those that Poe supports are ChatGPT and Claude, as shown to the left in Figure 10-11.

FIGURE 10-11: Poe-supported AI chatbots, AI models, and a tool to create a bot are listed in the toolbar.

Figure 10-12 shows the interface after you select the Create a Bot option from Poe's toolbar.

FIGURE 10-12: You can create your own chatbot by using an AI model available in Poe.

Quora states that Poe is the fastest interface for ChatGPT and that all the bots it supports are faster because of recent speed improvements to Poe. Poe is also the only consumer interface with Claude, which was developed by Anthropic, a startup company made of former OpenAI members who are seeking to build artificial general intelligence (AGI), the big AI of sci-fi lore.

Jasper

Jasper (formerly known as Jarvis) is an AI text-generation tool aimed at producing high-quality marketing and advertising copy and documents. The makers of Jasper recently created JasperChat, which is built on ChatGPT-3.5. They offer a free trial, but you have to enter a credit card to use it.

If you don't cancel your subscription after the free trial, your card is automatically charged $49 a month for Jasper's Business Plan and Boss Mode, which you use to reach JasperChat.

Figure 10-13 shows the Jasper setup screen for the free trial of both it and JasperChat.

FIGURE 10-13: Jasper and JasperChat are designed for marketing and advertising work.

Durable

Durable is an AI website builder tool. You can use Durable to build your website in about 30 seconds, complete with text, images, and customer testimonials. I'm not exaggerating.

It asked me for a business name (I made up *Scribblers*) and what my business does. On those two bits of information alone, Durable built me a website in less than 30 seconds. You can see part of that website in Figure 10-14.

FIGURE 10-14: Durable made a website for my fictional company in less than 30 seconds.

Like other generative AI models, if you're not happy with what it makes, just click Regenerate Response in whichever section you want it to redo.

And whoa, Durable even made up customer testimonials for my website, as you can see in Figure 10-15. That's not cool, but it's another example of why we should all be careful about assuming that AI-created content is truthful.

I had the pleasure of working with Scribblers Inc in Peachtree City, GA and was highly impressed with the quality of their content writing. They truly understand the importance of connecting with their target audience and were able to write compelling copy that was tailored to the needs of our business. Highly recommend!

– John L.

Our Clients

FIGURE 10-15: Whoa! Durable even made up some client testimonials for the website it made for me.

You can find Durable online at https://durable.co/ai-website-builder.

God Mode

No, God Mode doesn't have a direct connection to God nor is it a deity or demon. It's just another AI, but it does appear to work miracles. Give God Mode a goal, and it's off and running to do your bidding.

God Mode uses AutoGPT, ChatGPT's big brother, and you can find it online at https://godmode.space/. You'll need to sign in with a social media account or an OpenAI key.

Once you're in the system, God Mode can perform tasks for you on autopilot. Give it a task such as "find the cheapest price on the best performing TV available from anywhere in the US," as I did in Figure 10-16, and walk away. It'll figure out what it needs to find your answer all by itself.

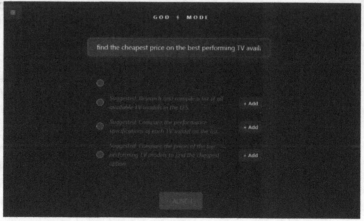

FIGURE 10-16: Give God Mode a task and it may suggest prompts or qualifiers to focus its task.

When God Mode is satisfied that it understands the task, it decides a plan to execute it, including establishing its reasoning and writing computer code, as shown in Figure 10-17. It will ask you to approve its plan first. Honestly, God Mode will blow your mind.

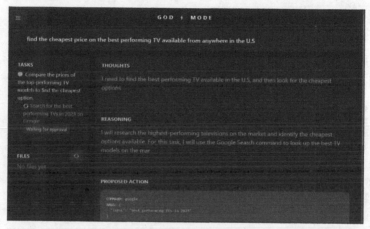

FIGURE 10-17: God Mode is an AI agent that sets out on a mission figuring out what to do as it goes and then executing each step automatically.

Index

Microsoft Bing, 101

Notion AI, 141

OpenAI API, 92

OpenAI Tokenizer tool, 56

OpenAI's GPT-4 Technical
Report, 65

prompt generator, 60

YouChat, 142

Weinberger, David (initiative
writer), 82–83

Wolfram, 68, 93

WolframAlpha, 123

word-in-computer (WIC)
analysis, 30

World Economic Forum, 74

World Intellectual Property
Organization (WIPO), 77

writing prompts, for ChatGPT,
47–60

Y

YouChat, 142–143

Z

Zapier, 68, 93

Zaremba, Wojciech (business
leader), 25

Zoom, 96

About the Author

Pam Baker is a veteran analyst, freelance journalist, and author. Her previous book, *Decision Intelligence For Dummies*, was also about AI. She writes for several media outlets, including *Institutional Investor*, Ars Technica, CIO, CISO, InformationWeek, CNN, *The New York Times*, PC magazine, The Economist Intelligence Unit, The Linux Foundation, TechTarget, and Dark Reading. She's the author of several previous books and a popular speaker at science and technology conferences. Her speech on mobile health data and analytics is published in the Annals of the New York Academy of Sciences. Former analyst engagements include research and reporting for ABI Research, VisionGain, and Evans Research. Pam is a member of the National Press Club (NPC), the Society of Professional Journalists (SPJ), and the Internet Press Guild (IPG). For her LinkedIn bio, references, and clips, go to www.linkedin.com/in/pambaker/.

Dedication

Dedicated to Stephanie Baker Forston and David Forston, Ben Baker and Dr. Katherine Poruk Baker, and my all inspiring and joy-infusing granddaughter crew: Mirabel, Coco, Poppy, and Charlotte. Special thanks to Ben for being my sounding board and technical adviser as I sorted out the details of the very new and incredibly fast-evolving ChatGPT. Thanks to Katherine for letting me use her office down by the sea. The two cats, Luna and Cinny, were an extra nice touch guys. Thanks to Stephanie for bringing your all every single time to every situation. To all of you, thanks for being my inspiration and support team through this and other writing marathons and for rocking my world.

Author's Acknowledgments

In the best of times, producing a book is a huge undertaking requiring many highly skilled and creative people to manifest the book in the real world. But this book pushed our collective and considerable skills to the limit given the newness of the technology and the speed in which it was evolving, as well as the crushing deadlines required to keep pace and produce a book worthy of our readers.

I offer my deepest gratitude to the many people who made this book possible and made it far better than I could have ever done alone.

A special thanks to Susan Pink, an editor worth her weight in gold and with a heart to match. Another huge thanks to the rest of the very talented editorial and production staff at Wiley. Many thanks also to Steven Hayes for making this book possible. And of course and always, a heartfelt thanks to my agent, Carole Jelen.

Publisher's Acknowledgments

Executive Editor: Steve Hayes

Senior Managing Editor:
Kristie Pyles

Project Editor: Susan Pink

Copy Editor: Susan Pink

Technical Editor: Rob Shimonski

Production Editor:
Tamilmani Varadharaj

Cover Image:
© Gorodenkoff/Shutterstock

Dummies is the global leader in the reference category and one of the most trusted and highly regarded brands in the world. No longer just focused on books, customers now have access to the dummies content they need in the format they want. Together we'll craft a solution that engages your customers, stands out from the competition, and helps you meet your goals.

Advertising & Sponsorships

Connect with an engaged audience on a powerful multimedia site, and position your message alongside expert how-to content. Dummies.com is a one-stop shop for free, online information and know-how curated by a team of experts.

- Targeted ads
- Video
- Email Marketing
- Microsites
- Sweepstakes sponsorship

20 MILLION PAGE VIEWS EVERY SINGLE MONTH

15 MILLION UNIQUE VISITORS PER MONTH

43% OF ALL VISITORS ACCESS THE SITE VIA THEIR MOBILE DEVICES

700,000 NEWSLETTER SUBSCRIPTIONS TO THE INBOXES OF

300,000 UNIQUE INDIVIDUALS EVERY WEEK

# of dummies

Custom Publishing

Reach a global audience in any language by creating a solution that will differentiate you from competitors, amplify your message, and encourage customers to make a buying decision.

- Apps
- Books
- eBooks
- Video
- Audio
- Webinars

Brand Licensing & Content

Leverage the strength of the world's most popular reference brand to reach new audiences and channels of distribution.

For more information, visit dummies.com/biz

PERSONAL ENRICHMENT

Staying Sharp
9781119187790
USA $26.00
CAN $31.99
UK £19.99

Facebook
9781119179030
USA $21.99
CAN $25.99
UK £16.99

Guitar
9781119293354
USA $24.99
CAN $29.99
UK £17.99

Investing
9781119293347
USA $22.99
CAN $27.99
UK £16.99

Beekeeping
9781119310068
USA $22.99
CAN $27.99
UK £16.99

Digital Photography
9781119235606
USA $24.99
CAN $29.99
UK £17.99

Meditation
9781119251163
USA $24.99
CAN $29.99
UK £17.99

Pregnancy
9781119235491
USA $26.99
CAN $31.99
UK £19.99

Samsung Galaxy S7
9781119279952
USA $24.99
CAN $29.99
UK £17.99

iPhone
9781119283133
USA $24.99
CAN $29.99
UK £17.99

Crocheting
9781119287117
USA $24.99
CAN $29.99
UK £16.99

Nutrition
9781119130246
USA $22.99
CAN $27.99
UK £16.99

PROFESSIONAL DEVELOPMENT

Windows 10
9781119311041
USA $24.99
CAN $29.99
UK £17.99

AutoCAD
9781119255796
USA $39.99
CAN $47.99
UK £27.99

Excel 2016
9781119293439
USA $26.99
CAN $31.99
UK £19.99

QuickBooks 2017
9781119281467
USA $26.99
CAN $31.99
UK £19.99

macOS Sierra
9781119280651
USA $29.99
CAN $35.99
UK £21.99

LinkedIn
9781119251132
USA $24.99
CAN $29.99
UK £17.99

Windows 10
9781119310563
USA $34.00
CAN $41.99
UK £24.99

SharePoint 2016
9781119181705
USA $29.99
CAN $35.99
UK £21.99

Fundamental Analysis
9781119263593
USA $26.99
CAN $31.99
UK £19.99

Networking
9781119257769
USA $29.99
CAN $35.99
UK £21.99

Office 2016
9781119293477
USA $26.99
CAN $31.99
UK £19.99

Office 365
9781119265313
USA $24.99
CAN $29.99
UK £17.99

Salesforce.com
9781119239314
USA $29.99
CAN $35.99
UK £21.99

Coding
9781119293323
USA $29.99
CAN $35.99
UK £21.99

dummies.com

dummies
A Wiley Brand